THE ECONOMIC & SOCIAL BENEFITS OF

STOCK MARKETS

IT'S NO GAMBLE

THE ECONOMIC & SOCIAL BENEFITS OF
STOCK MARKETS

IT'S NO GAMBLE

Lewis D. Johnson & Bohumír Pazderka

THE FRASER INSTITUTE

The authors of this book have worked independently and opinions expressed by them, therefore, are their own, and do not necessarily reflect the opinions of the members or the trustees of The Fraser Institute.

Printed in Canada.

Canadian Cataloguing in Publication Data

Johnson, Lewis David, 1948–
It's no gamble

Includes bibliographical references.
ISBN 0-88975-174-9

1. Stock exchange. 2. Stock-exchange—Canada. 3. Speculation. I. Pazderka, Bohumír, 1941– II. Fraser Institute (Vancouver, B.C.) III. Title.

HG4551.J63 1995 332.64 C95-910259-0

Contents

List of Tables

List of Figures

Preface

SOMETIMES GREAT IDEAS PASS US BY because they seem ordinary. The Yale lock, the zipper, and the paper clip are brilliant inventions we take for granted. The stock market also belongs in this class. It has made Canada wealthy and secure. But few people would place the stock market high on the list of this century's great achievements. All those angry-looking men shouting at each other on the trading floor to sell, or buy, or do whatever it takes to turn a buck, do not inspire admiration. It has taken researchers many years to understand that there is science behind the shouting; a science that works for ordinary Canadians as surely as nuclear reactors keep them warm and computers make them good at their work.

Most of us do not share these researchers' insights. What we hear comes from the media, which tells a sordid story of greed and vanity: Stock markets are like a casino. Money changes hands but nothing of value gets made. What I win comes at your loss. Speculators make prices jump about and leave the world a less stable place. Ruthless corporate raiders use the stock market to raise money for unethical leveraged buyouts, and inside traders use it to fleece ignorant stockholders. In this jungle investors go for the quick gain and neglect worthy companies with long-term plans.

Scare stories are easy to write but they lack perspective. The present book by Professors Lewis Johnson and Bohumir Pazderka of Queen's University School of Business brings us closer to the truth about stock markets and restores balance to the discussion of this much maligned institution. These experts delve into scholarly research of the past 20 years to explain, in simple terms, that stock markets bring benefits to Canadian society. What follows is an outline of the thoughtful and well-researched ideas Professors Johnson and Pazderka consider.

The search for value

Stock markets spread risks, raise capital, direct information to its best use, and keep managers efficient and loyal. These functions may not grab the headlines, but that is perhaps because the headlines are missing the point. The stock market has evolved to answer one of the most basic questions that humans ask: "How much is it worth?" While philosophers debate what is important and valuable in life, financiers and traders put their money on the line to find the answer.

The inventor of a new antibiotic who forms a company may need the money of others to bring his product to the world. To get this money he can sell stock. He puts his idea on the auction block, where other financial experts will focus their expertise on setting a price. These other experts are investors or their talented agents. Investors will set the right price for the stock if they assess correctly how much good the antibiotic will do, and how much it will cost to make the antibiotic. If investors fail to see the full benefit of the drug they will bid too low and the company develops more slowly than it might have. If investors overestimate the benefit of the drug they neglect to put their money in other projects which consumers value more highly. In either case, the mistake is costly.

A great university

The risk of bearing these costs sharpens the mind and pushes investors to make use of every scrap of information they can get their hands on. Nothing goes to waste. Once a company is on the road, investors keep a close watch for any new information that may surface. Can the drug be improved? Are consumers satisfied? If investors are doing their jobs well, the moment news arrives the price of the stock will change to reflect that news. Because information has a way of turning up randomly we would expect stock prices in an efficient market to behave randomly. The whimsical rise and fall of the stock exchange does not reflect indecision or financial manipulations. The flutter of the TSE shows that investors are making good use of the truths that nature uncovers according to her fancy. Louis Pasteur told his students that chance favours the prepared mind. Investors spend billions of dollars preparing their minds for nature's revelations. These outlays on "turning a buck" have made stock markets into centres of learning that stand equal to the world's great universities. The difference between the two enterprises is that professors can afford to indulge in research about which few people care. Investors in a well-regulated market must seek the greatest good of the greatest number of people. Seeking this greatest good is the way to riches.

"Protect us from all anxiety"

One of the finest fruits of stock market research has been the discovery that bundles of stocks and bonds can protect people from risk. These bundles are known as diversified portfolios and derivative securities (or simply "derivatives"). Derivatives are securities that derive their value from some underlying security such as a stock, a commodity, or a currency. The best known derivatives are options. A type of option known as a put allows you to sell stock, commodities, or currency at a guaranteed price, for a guaranteed number of months. If the Canadian dollar is at 75 cents U.S. and I fear that it will fall to 70 cents in the next six months I can buy a put that will give me the right to sell each of 100,000 Canadian dollars for 75 cents U.S. This is particularly handy if my construction business imports its shingles from the U.S. A fall in the Canadian dollar could raise my costs at home and put me out of business. The put is also handy if I am a pensioner with my life savings in Canadian assets and I am tired of seeing these assets shrink every time our dollar falls.

The beauty of options is that I do not have to hold $100,000 Canadian to sell $100,000. I simply buy the right to sell the dollars at a guaranteed price. I buy this right from someone in the market who thinks that the Canadian dollar is not going to fall. I can think of him as my insurance agent, though he may be a rancher in Alberta or a merchant banker in Japan. If my fears about a currency disaster were wrong, this insurance agent makes his commission of a few hundred dollars. If my disaster happens he picks up what may turn out to be a very large tab. Millions of insurance policies such as these sell every day.

Shuttling risk around

The derivatives market allows people who can tolerate risk and who have a good sense of where real risk lies to take a weight of worry off the minds of more timid investors. Timidity takes many forms. Some people may fear that prices will either rise or fall, or that prices will not change, or that prices will rise then fall. The derivative's market has an "instrument" to protect against all patterns of risk. The design of these financial instruments is a science that works for the good of mankind. The peace of mind that financial scientists sell encourages timid investors to bring their funds to the stock market. This widens the pool of capital that feeds a nation's growth.

Derivatives make fine insurance because they can derive from almost any worrisome feature of the underlying security. If the investor fears, for some reason, that the Canadian dollar will stay within a two cent range of its present value, a derivative can be fashioned to protect him. Derivatives allow investors to do away with the possibilities they do not like about the underlying securities. Derivatives unpack the mixed bag of fortune and failure people get when they are buying something like a stock. Unpacking is good because it widens the choices people can make. For example, if music lovers could tailor a CD to their tastes they would save themselves the expense of buying many records with only a few pieces they want to hear.

Easy to misunderstand

Sometimes insurers will make large mistakes, and be forced to pay out painful sums to the people who bought their derivatives. These are occasions for the media to whoop with indignation. In an October 1994 feature, *Time* magazine drew attention to recent losses by mutual funds. These funds had put too much of their money in derivatives. *Time* primly declared that it had "Warned earlier this year . . . that derivatives posed a new and little understood threat to U.S. consumers and companies." The article painted a heartbreaking picture of innocent people lying broken under the "financial wreckage" done by derivatives. The main lack of understanding however was with the *Time* reporter, who seemed ignorant of the simplest facts about derivatives' markets. The only people who can be broken in these markets are the risk-takers who sell the insurance. Their loss is balanced by the gains of timid investors who buy derivatives as protection against financial shocks. If reporters do not lament the life insurance money that Allstate pays to bereaved families, then reporters should dry their tears for the derivatives' sellers who take risks and pay the price.

The media are just now discovering that derivatives exist, so perhaps their weak grasp of the issues and their isolation from academic findings should not surprise us. For example, painstaking studies by prominent U.S. economists and by the O.E.C.D. conclude that in the 20 years since derivatives became big business, financial markets have not become less stable. This may be hard to digest for those, such as *Fortune* reporter Carol Loomis who trumpet that derivatives have put the world's "financial system" in danger. To find likelier causes of risk in our society we do not need to look for exotic financial explanations. Something much more ordinary may be to blame.

The honourable crapshooter

Ironically, government may be to thank for the turning the stock market into a supermarket for insurance. One of the intellectual excuses for the explosion of government that started in the 1930s was that the state had a duty to insulate the economy from violent ups and downs. By spending heavily when the economy was depressed and by spending little when the economy boomed government was going to iron out the peaks and troughs of economic fate. Careful regulation of the financial system would keep banks and trusts from speculating with other peoples' money and going under, while the bank of Canada kept the currency steady. This intellectual apology for big government won applause, even though history teaches that concentrating power in a few hands can make the future uncertain. Since the 1930s government has done much to destabilize the economy. Our large debt scares away investors who fear that the taxman may call on them to pay it down. The Bank of Canada plays roulette with inflation by refusing to follow strict rules about how the money supply will grow. And everywhere the government insulates people from the consequences of making risky decisions. Bailouts for businesses encourage excessively daring investments, and unemployment insurance relieves workers of looking for jobs where the risk of being laid off is low. Perhaps investors have turned to stock markets as a way of taming the risks that governments set loose. In taming risk the stock market is fulfilling the promise of stability that the welfare state has failed to keep.

The good speculator

It may seem odd to think of the stock market as a place where people put a price on their ignorance and buy relief from the anxiety it brings. We are more at home with the notion of the stock market as a terrain where reckless speculators and arbitrageurs trade on their hunches and destabilize prices. The media encourage this notion because it makes for easy and sensational reporting. The good deeds that speculators and arbitrageurs do are harder to understand.

Speculators are in the business of buying up goods or materials in times of plenty and selling them in times of need. This saves us from living either in feast or famine. For his services to society the speculator has earned money and a bad name stretching back thousands of years. Roman historians record that in 67 B.C. pirates infested the Mediterranean and cut off the corn supply to Italy. These historians thought it was obvious that speculators held on to their supplies of corn to drive up the price. They did not ponder that if speculators had not held on to their supplies there would have been no corn left for the catastrophic times that many believed lay ahead (as it happened, Pompey the Great took command of a Roman fleet, made short work of the pirates, and sent corn prices plunging, but that is not the point of the story).

When a speculator today buys stock in a drug company he is betting that in the future there will be a strong demand for the drug. His investment helps the company survive until the day when consumers have the greatest need for the company's particular expertise. When the speculator sells the company short, he is guessing that someday few people will need the drug. Maybe something better is being developed that will make the company obsolete. A short sale allows the speculator to take resources out of the company and invest them where he thinks they will be most needed.

The work of speculators also stabilizes prices over time. Buying today on a hunch that prices will rise tomorrow, makes prices today rise. Setting aside supplies for tomorrow means that the price rise in the future will not be as great as speculators at first anticipate. In other words, speculators can help to spread the shock of a future price increase back to the present, so that the future shock is not so great. Of course, when speculators are wrong, they can destabilize prices. Speculators who are wrong on average, however, do not stay in the business for very long.

The efficiency of arbitrage

Arbitrageurs are in the business of finding a single resource that sells for two prices. Suppose eggs sell for $1 a dozen in the supermarket and for $2 a dozen in the open air market across town. This is a bad situation because it means that there is a needless shortage of eggs in the outside market. The arbitrageur will make money if he buys as much as he can from the supermarket and sells it outside. His search for profits will bring eggs to where consumers need them most and will force merchants in both markets to bring their prices in line with each other.

Arbitrageurs perform the same social service that speculators perform. The only difference is that speculators move resources between the present and the future. Arbitrageurs move resources from place to place. Recognizing an opportunity for arbitrage becomes complicated when the resource in question is a stock, or even a portfolio of stocks and bonds. Two portfolios that do not have a single stock or bond in common may really be no different from the other. What matters to investors is the pattern of returns the portfolios promise. The trick is to identify portfolios that sell for different prices but promise the same returns under the same conditions of risk. An arbitrageur may discover that pensioners are paying too much for their retirement portfolio. A different and cheaper combination of stocks and bonds could sustain pensioners in the same style the old portfolio promised. The arbitrageur performs a social service by bringing cheaper alternatives to the attention of people who might be interested.

Leveraged buyouts and democracy

The profound interest that investors, speculators, and arbitrageurs have in making money has turned the stock market into a refined democracy. Every time they buy or sell a stock they cast a vote for or against the company. Company managers face a sobering opinion poll every day. If people are selling stock because the managers are incompetent, someone may scoop up a majority of stocks, win control of the company, and throw out the managers. This "someone" is usually an investor who has studied the company, and thinks he understands its true potential. By using financial instruments such as junk bonds, the investor can raise the capital he needs to buy out a mismanaged, undervalued company.

The use of junk bonds to finance leveraged buyouts became a science in the 1980s, under the intellectual leadership of Wall Street financier Michael Milken. Milken saw that there were pools of credit that could be tapped to bring value back to badly run enterprises. This discovery brought a just balance of power to shareholders suffering under wayward managers. Milken made a fortune selling his socially valuable service but excited such jealousy and suspicion that he was thrown in prison.

Baking a bigger pie

The people who play the stock market may not realize it, but they are helping to build the nation. When investors sink time and money into researching which companies will grow, they are helping to guide resources to their best use. Betting a company will grow fast means putting funds at its disposal. It also means holding back funds from other companies with less chance of growing. By moving resources where they will be most productive, stock markets help to drive economic growth. Stock markets are not about slicing the pie. They are about baking a bigger pie.

Eastern European economies are a refreshing reminder of how important it is to have an organized market for financial securities. When governments in the East decided that it was time to privatize industry they faced a problem: At what price should these industries sell? The Czech Republic led the way by suggesting that private citizens should decide. The state entitled each Czech to a small share of the industries the state was privatizing. Citizens put about 70 percent of these shares (called vouchers) in the care of investment fund managers. Managers started trading these vouchers and soon it emerged that some industries sold for more vouchers than others. These different values grew out of the market research that the investment fund managers had done on behalf of their clients. This first act in the Czech economic play revealed where the country's best prospects lay.

The Czech experience is also a reminder of why investment funds are good for us. In the last decade they have become important traders on the world's exchanges. Investment funds are popular because they give ordinary people the chance to invest a few thousand dollars each year without having to become market experts. The funds take it on themselves to become the experts. They specialize in gathering information about the market and pass the benefits of this specialization on to their clients.

Regulations needed

For any kind of market to work it helps to have regulations that punish dishonesty and protect consumers, without limiting the useful choices these consumers can make. The stock market is not perfect and can sometimes hurt those who use it, as Professors Johnson and Pazderka document. However, in their zeal to protect the people who buy financial products, government should make sure that it is not really blocking a productive exchange of resources. The recent push by G-7 countries to limit or even eliminate trade in derivatives is an example of misguided zeal. Sound regulations will only come from people who understand what is good in the stock market. This is no simple matter because stock markets are complicated and it takes an educated eye to appreciate their subtle workings. As ecologists have shown, you do not protect a forest from fire by stamping out every blaze the moment it starts. Sometimes the best policy is to let the forest burn a while. Forest management is a scientific business that follows rules which are not obvious at first sight. Professors Johnson and Pazderka explain that we should be open to similar possibilities when it comes to stock markets.

—Filip Palda

Acknowledgements

WE WOULD LIKE TO ACKNOWLEDGE the inspiration and dedication of Dr. Filip Palda, whose thoughtful, insightful, and firm editing contributed to a much better book. Among our colleagues, Louis Gagnon, Kristian Palda, and Vladimir Popov offered helpful comments. Our understanding of the problems of corporate governance has benefited from discussions and joint work with Ted Neave. We also wish to acknowledge the reference assistance of Scott Allerston and Sheila Johnson, and the research assistance of Nadine Anderson and Natalie Trevithick.

The Canadian investment community owes a deep debt of gratitude to Keith Ambachtsheer for his vision and perseverance in initiating *Canadian Investment Review*. A casual glance at the bibliography to this book will confirm CIR's importance as a forum for discussion of investment topics in Canada.

About the Authors

Lewis D. Johnson

Lew Johnson is a Professor at the School of Business, Queen's University, where he teaches undergraduate and graduate courses in investments and corporate finance. He is a graduate of the University of New Brunswick, Dalhousie University, Saint Mary's University, and the University of Toronto (where he received his Ph.D.).

Professor Johnson's research activities have principally focused on the valuation of financial assets and the operation of financial markets. He has published widely in academic and professional journals, and is a frequent commentator to the media about financial affairs.

Bohumír Pazderka

Bohumír Pazderka is an Associate Professor at the School of Business, Queen's University, where he teaches microeconomics and business-government relations. Born in Czechoslovakia, he graduated from the School of Economics in Bratislava and later obtained his Ph.D. from Queen's University.

Professor Pazderka's research interests include the economics of the pharmaceutical industry and the health care system, and the economics of research and development and innovation. He has done consulting work for various departments of the government of Canada and the province of Ontario, and has collaborated with the Thailand Development Research Institute in Bangkok. Recently, he has developed an interest in the problems of transition of the former centrally planned economies of eastern Europe to a market system and has given a number of lectures at the University of Economics in Slovakia.

Professor Pazderka has co-authored a textbook and two monographs, and has published a number of articles in academic journals. His most recent publication, with Professor Johnson, appeared in *Managerial and Decision Economics.*

Dedication

To our families.

Introduction

Stock markets and the economy

FEW INSTITUTIONS ARE AS MALIGNED and misunderstood as the stock market. Financial markets in general are seen by many as a visible symbol of the greed and financial excesses of the 1980s—witness such popular books as *Liar's Poker* (Lewis 1989) and *Bonfire of the Vanities* (Wolfe 1987). Stock markets in particular are seen by some as speculative gambles at best and manipulated private clubs at worst. This latter view, espoused, for example, by Canadian writer Walter Stewart (1992),[1] gains prominence whenever evidence of market corruption gets media attention and lobbyists call for the imposition of stricter regulation. Others, such as international business guru Michael Porter (1992), blame the decline of North American competitiveness on myopic stock market investors who, the story goes, exert pressure on corporate management to pursue short-term profits at the expense of long-term strategic planning.

The purpose of this book is to look at how stock markets help economic growth and development, and to weigh the evidence about how well they discharge this function. We argue that stock markets are a vital intermediary in an industrial economy, facilitating the pooling of funds, the sharing of risks, and the transfer of wealth. Without them,

---

1 *The Golden Fleece* vilifies Canadian stock markets. Analogous treatments of Wall Street are proffered in Elias (1971), Ney (1970), and Baruch (1971), among others. For a more sympathetic view of Bay Street, see Ross (1984).

resources would not flow to the most productive investment opportunities, and economic growth would suffer. Indeed, with trade barriers loosening around the world, a country's very economic survival may depend on well-functioning stock markets.

The following quote gives an indication of the range of tasks that the stock market is expected to perform:

> The stock market is more than a place where traders buy and sell bits and pieces of corporate ownership. It is more than an outlet for our savings or a source of finance for corporations seeking more capital. It is more than an instrument for valuing giant corporations. It is more than a means for transforming fixed capital assets into a liquid form that can be converted into cash. (Bernstein 1992b, p. 298)

Indeed, the stock market plays an important role in the daily economic life of this country. We hope to make a contribution toward a better understanding of how the stock market fulfils this role, and thus to foster a deeper appreciation of its economic importance. To accomplish this task, we draw upon a large body of theoretical literature and review the empirical evidence on the social benefits of stock markets. We pay special—but not exclusive—attention to the Canadian scene.

This book also attempts to correct some of the myths and misconceptions regarding the stock market. These myths have a powerful hold on people who criticize the stock market and on those who call for increased government regulation.

Myth 1

Stock markets are a zero-sum game; namely, what one person wins has to come at somebody else's loss. Walter Stewart (1992) is an important proponent of this view. He alleges that stock markets are merely a "crap game" in which the small investor is invariably cheated by those in the know. Table 1 demonstrates that investing in the stock market over long periods provides superior returns to investing in bonds, and that those returns are sufficient to beat inflation. As the economy grows, so does the total value of all the stocks outstanding. Some, of course, give better returns than others, and some decline in value. Moreover, some (mainly small) investors do get hurt by broker malfeasance (see chapter 7), but

Table 1: Capital Market Rates of Return in Canada, 1926-1993 (Percent)

	1926-1949	1950-1993	1926-1993
A. *Nominal rates of return*			
Common stocks	7.4	10.9	9.6
Long term govt. bonds	4.7	6.5	5.8
Difference	2.7	4.4	3.8
B. *Change in Consumer Price Index*	1.1	4.5	3.3
C. *Inflation-adjusted (i.e., real) rates of return*			
Common stocks	6.3	6.3	6.3
Long term govt. bonds	3.6	1.9	2.5
Difference	2.7	4.4	3.8

Sources: 1926-1949: Canadian Institute of Actuaries, "Report on Canadian Economic Statistics," table 1, page 2.
1950-1987: Hatch & White, "Canadian Stocks, Bonds, Bills and Inflation: 1950-1987," table 5-1, page 110.
1988-1992: Canadian Institute of Actuaries, "Report on Canadian Economic Statistics," table 1, page 2.
1993: Toronto Stock Exchange; ScotiaMcLeod Debt Market Indices; and Statistics Canada.

that does not invalidate the attractiveness of long-term investment in stocks, even for small investors.[2]

Stewart supports his accusations with a litany of examples where small stockholders have been disadvantaged, and, as the "coup-de-grâce," refers to the existence of instruments such as the Toronto Index Participation Units (TIPs), a security which tracks the value of the TSE 35 Index:

2 We emphasize "long-term" returns here, because, as is well known, the stock market can be a dangerous place for investments in the short run (such as in October 1987).

> None of these dice-rolling instruments has anything to do with bankrolling enterprise or participating in decision-making or, indeed, anything to do with anything but shouting, "Baby needs a new pair of shoes!" and praying not to roll craps. (p. 8)

While such prose is graphic and eye-catching, it unfortunately displays a simple-minded naivety regarding the operation of the stock market. The role of TIPs in allowing investors to hedge risk is explained in chapter 1.

Myth 2

The stock market is a source of economic instability. Supposedly, market volatility has increased with the growth of trading in so-called "derivatives" such as options and futures contracts. According to the critics, trading in derivatives has introduced to the market a "systemic" risk, meaning that the failure of one institution could bring down the entire financial system like a house of cards. Stewart (1992) dismisses derivative securities as mere "bets," and again shows a lack of appreciation of their role in reducing risks and thus facilitating economic development (which we explore in chapter 1).

Myth 3

People who "play" stock markets demand a quick return on their money and ignore long-term investments. Institutional investors are particularly maligned for their "bottom line" mentality. Michael Porter (1992) may have been partly right in criticizing the role of myopic investors in corporate strategic planning, but as we discuss in chapter 7, much of that kind of behaviour is changing as institutional investors take a more active role as "relationship investors," becoming long-term partners in the enterprise and taking a longer-term perspective.

Myth 4

Much financial system activity is mere "paper shuffling" that has nothing to do with the creation of real wealth. Critics often point to mergers and acquisitions and to "junk bonds" as prime examples of this allegation. We show in chapter 3 that mergers and acquisitions add to economic growth, and that junk bonds and other financial innovations are important contributors to this process. Corporate reorganization is part of the natural evolution of a company, and mergers and acquisitions serve to reduce inefficiency: the surviving company is usually better able to compete effectively than could the pre-takeover entities.

Myth 5

Stock market investors risk losing their money to firms that lie about their prospects when issuing new stock. A more realistic perspective is to view stock markets as a giant laboratory where investors try to find the best mix of stocks for their purposes. Finding this mix is expensive because the investor must research potential investments and weigh the information a company puts out about itself against his or her previous experience with the company. The stock market is driven by a search for information about which investments deserve a try, and which investments are likely to fail, and many companies specialize in collecting and selling information about investment prospects. We discuss the efficiency with which stock markets process such information in chapter 4.

Other myths and misconceptions about the stock market abound, and we debunk some of them throughout the book. We hope to leave the reader with a more informed opinion of the stock market, which will allow him or her to separate myth from reality.

We begin with a history of the development of stock markets and an examination of their structure and functions in chapter 1. We describe the creation of new market instruments such as derivative securities (so called because their value derives from that of an underlying asset), and examine objectively their role in fostering economic growth. Such objectivity has been largely absent from most media reports on derivatives. The central function of the stock market is to act as "middleman" between investors and public companies, and we describe its role in accommodating the different attitudes of individual investors to risk and their needs for a variety of forms of income, while at the same time ensuring that funds flow to the most profitable investment opportunities.

The stock market acts as a link between investors and company management. It allows managers to know what investors want and it allows investors to control their managers. Chapters 2 and 3 examine several aspects of the stock market's role in corporate governance. Chapter 2 focuses on the consequences of separation of ownership and control in shareholder-owned corporations (i.e., the managers of large companies tend not to be major shareholders, and they may have goals different from those of the owners), and on differential voting shares (i.e., shares with different voting power). Both of these features are frequently considered to work to the disadvantage of investors (particularly small investors). Managers are presumed to have motives different from those of the owners (investors), and, if left unconstrained, will manage a company in their own interests at the expense of the owners. We review the monitoring roles of the board of directors and institutional investors, and conclude that Canadian companies are comparable to those in the U.S., but the ability of managers to pursue their own goals may place Canadian companies at a (shrinking) competitive disadvantage relative to Japanese and German competitors.

Differential voting shares pose a different problem. The conflict here is between different classes of shareholders, not between managers and shareholders (although there could be some overlap in these categories). One group of shareholders—one that holds a disproportionate number of votes per share—is able to wield power far in excess of its monetary stake in the company. Increasing institutional involvement in corporate governance is redressing a part of the power imbalance, as large institutional investors are taking a larger role at shareholder meetings and on boards of directors. The stock market also serves to redress the imbalance, as voting and non-voting (or lesser-voting) shares are priced at different levels, reflecting the value of different degrees of control.

Although the influence investors exercise through voting at shareholder meetings and through representation on boards of directors does constrain the behaviour of managers, considerable scope for managerial discretion remains, and some companies are undervalued because of managerial action or inaction. A class of investors, called "corporate raiders," specializes in identifying, or targeting, corporations whose market value and shareholder returns could be improved if existing management were replaced. These raiders are often maligned in the press but perform a vital disciplining function. Chapter 3 explains how they use the facilities of the stock market to engineer a takeover of target corporations—called a "hostile takeover" if opposed by incumbent owners and managers. In successful takeovers, the surviving company is often reorganized and streamlined, leading to its more efficient operation. The financial instruments used in the process include the much maligned "junk bonds" (low-grade securities with high degrees of risk). We discuss the role of the stock market in accomplishing takeovers and review the empirical evidence on the contribution of takeovers to the efficiency and competitiveness of the economy.

Chapter 4 explains the complicated concept of stock market efficiency. Efficiency has several meanings that critics of the stock market often confuse. We address two aspects of efficiency: does the market fairly price stocks (i.e., does price reflect value), and does the market do so at a reasonable cost (i.e., are transaction costs so high as to hinder efficient trading)? We conclude that Canadian markets are just as efficient as U.S. markets but may be less efficient than those of Japan and Europe. We also note the importance of investor confidence in the capital formation process: investors are loath to give their hard-earned money to strangers if they do not trust the process. Investor trust is the motivation behind much of the government regulation of the stock market, as we explore in chapter 7.

In chapter 5, we offer an additional perspective on the vital importance of stock markets in modern economies. We refer here to the spectacular development of stock markets in the former centrally-planned economies of eastern Europe, and in emerging markets elsewhere. There are, of course, questions and doubts, and we address them in our discussion of the comparative effectiveness of allocating financial resources through stock markets or through the banking system, which is the stock market's major competitor in financial markets around the world. In a broader context, this debate ties in with our analysis of corporate governance in chapter 2, and the relative merits of the "stock market-based" financial systems of Canada and the U.S. versus the "bank-based" systems of Continental Europe and Japan.

Chapter 6 tackles selected ethical issues related to the functioning of stock markets, including the morality of defensive measures in the face of hostile takeovers, the moral defensibility of insider trading (trades of stock by those with inside information, such as management, auditors, and lawyers), and the role of corporate social responsibility. All of these issues have been extensively—but not always objectively—treated in popular writings critical of the stock market. The market does a much better job of enforcing morality than many people think. We draw upon selected concepts in philosophy and ethics in an attempt to offer a framework for formulating an individual attitude toward this key institution of capitalism.

The book concludes with a discussion of public policy issues and stock market regulation. We consider the evidence on allegations of market failure and moral failure and evaluate the current system of self-regulation against the background of the market's performance and the imperative of investor confidence in the capital formation process. Drawing on the current regulatory reform of public utilities as an analogy, we determine that the restrictions placed on stock market activity should reflect underlying competitive conditions. Competition in this case means that all investors have equal access to accurate information on companies, with competitive activity taking the form of researching and processing information. Some (mostly larger) investors are better able to conduct such research than smaller investors, and some (mostly larger) companies have such information more readily available. As well, these larger investors tend to concentrate their investments in these larger companies. We recognize, then, that there are two distinct types of market: the "upper tier" dominated by larger sophisticated investors, and a "lower tier" populated by small, less well-informed investors. We conclude that a revised, two-tier form of market regulation, with the upper tier largely unregulated, would probably best serve the goal of developing a competitive economy with a broadly-based participation of Canadians in the financing of its growth and the benefits derived from it.

Chapter 1: The Structure and Role of Stock Markets

MANY OF THE MYTHS surrounding the stock market result from a lack of understanding of its structure and function. This chapter first reviews the history and development of stock markets, and introduces some of its innovative features, such as the creation of derivative securities. We then explain how stock markets bring together companies and investors and accommodate their particular needs, such as different degrees of risk tolerance. Finally, we discuss several trends in the functioning of stock markets. Canadian stock markets have been world leaders in implementing modern techniques and technologies of trading. This evolution has occurred because of dynamic entrepreneurial leadership; further evolution requires similar leadership and vision by both market leaders and by governments, which must refrain from unduly burdening the exchanges in the global marketplace.

A brief history

Why do we need markets? A market is simply a central trading post. Markets for goods first developed in primitive economies, when division of labour (hunting, fishing, farming, et cetera) led to the need for a means to exchange goods. Pre-industrial markets were largely agricultural, and towns served as central market places for surrounding farms. The industrial age saw a further division of labour, since whole families were employed in non-agrarian activities and little time was available for production of household goods (such as furniture and clothing), which were much cheaper when produced by machines at any rate. This led to the growth of larger and more diverse markets as society became increasingly urbanized.

Industrialization also required a market for capital. In simpler times, personal resources and local institutions were adequate to finance small enterprises, but the larger scale of industrial activities needed capital from other, more "distant" sources. Common stocks[3] developed as a vehicle to facilitate such capital acquisition. They provided a mechanism whereby funds could be pooled and risks shared by numerous "arm's-length" participants, freeing the entrepreneur from the limitations imposed by the size of his or her personal wealth.

Stock trading appears to have first taken place in Antwerp in 1602, and developed into an exchange at Amsterdam in 1611 (Cooke, 1969, p. 305). Over-the-counter markets developed in England in the latter half of the sixteenth century,[4] and in 1773 the London Stock Exchange was founded. The Paris Bourse was founded in 1726, but it too had been preceded by less formal stock brokerage businesses, possibly as early as at the beginning of the fourteenth century (Dice, 1926, p. 131).

In North America, organized stock trading began in 1790 with the precursor to the Philadelphia-Baltimore-Washington Stock Exchange. Two years later, the "Buttonwood Tree Agreement" formalized the activities of stock brokers in New York City, and led to the formation of the New York Stock Exchange in 1817 (Cooke, 1969, p. 307). The American Stock Exchange began with outdoor trading in 1849 (hence its moniker "the Curb"), and moved indoors finally in 1921. Later, a

---

3 The term "stock" derives from the French term "souche" (stub or stump of a tree trunk), and refers to the stick or tally upon which debts and claims were notched (OED).

4 Over-the-counter markets are informal networks of traders, in contrast to the organized exchanges, which are physical market-places.

number of local and regional exchanges were started, the most prominent being the Midwest (now Chicago) and Pacific Stock Exchanges.

Organized share trading in Canada began in Montreal in 1832 in the Exchange Coffee House, later, in 1874, to become the Montreal Stock Exchange (Hatch and Robinson 1989, 229). The Montreal Stock Exchange merged in 1974 with the Canadian Stock Exchange, which had been founded in 1926 as the Montreal Curb Market, to deal with more speculative issues. The current name is the Montreal Exchange, reflecting the wider variety of securities, other than common stocks, on offer.

The Toronto Stock Exchange began informally in 1852 and was incorporated in 1878. In 1934, it merged with the Standard Stock and Mining Exchange, which, in turn, grew out of a merger with the Toronto Mining and Industrial Exchange, both specializing in the trading of mining stocks.

While the Toronto and Montreal exchanges traded in shares of more established firms, the Vancouver Stock Exchange, incorporated in 1907, focused on more speculative, start-up situations—"the venture capital capital," as it styles itself. Its orientation has always been on resource-based firms, but high technology companies are currently in vogue as well, along with an outreach program for new Asian listings.

The Calgary Stock Exchange was formed in 1914, and changed its name to the Alberta Stock Exchange in 1974. It has historically served as a regional, resource-based market, but has also branched out into non-resource instruments, principally (during the late 1980s) the so-called "blind pools" or "nickel stocks."[5]

The Winnipeg Stock Exchange, founded in 1904, serves primarily as a regulator, with very little active trading (there is no trading floor). The Edmonton Stock Exchange is now defunct. There is an exchange

---

5 These instruments were designed by the Alberta Government to stimulate local entrepreneurial investment. Initially, they sold for five cents a share ("nickel share") and did not require a detailed prospectus on planned investment activity ("blind pool"). Abuse of these weak reporting requirements later led to more stringent regulation. Robinson (1993a) provides a history of this program.

authorized in Halifax, but it remains inactive pending further development of the Hibernia offshore oil fields.

Structure of the stock market

Stock markets compete actively with one another for business. Table 2 displays the dollar value and volume of trading in 1992 and 1993 for the major North American exchanges. The New York Stock Exchange is clearly the dominant North American market, but Toronto compares favourably in both value and volume. Vancouver ranks third on volume but only tenth on value, reflecting the predominance of penny stocks traded on that exchange. Montreal and Alberta have both recently moved up the list in volume terms, while the Winnipeg totals, as might be expected, are minuscule.

The exchanges are all physical market places (although, as noted, Winnipeg has no trading floor). In contrast, the over-the-counter (OTC) markets[6] are electronic, and all trading is conducted by telephone or, increasingly, by computer.[7] The major U.S. OTC market is NASDAQ (National Association of Securities Dealers Automated Quotation system). In Canada, the principal OTC market is the Canadian Dealer Network (CDN), a subsidiary of the Toronto Stock Exchange. Stocks traded over the counter tend to be those of smaller and less mature companies than the exchange-listed stocks (because of the exchanges' listing requirements, which require timely and full disclosure of significant events), but they may also be stocks of larger, established companies wanting privacy, which may not be consistent with the exchanges' disclosure requirements.

Stock trading takes place in the primary market or in the secondary market. Stocks are initially offered to the public in the primary market,

---

6 Their name derived from the practice of banks in earlier times selling securities literally "over the counter."

7 However, as discussed later, this distinction is blurring, as more exchanges replace the traditional "open outcry" floor trading system with electronic trading.

Table 2: North American Stock Market Trading

Annual Value (in Thousands of Canadian Dollars)		
Exchange	**1993**	**1992**
New York	3,035,081,456	2,214,995,862
Toronto	147,055,049	76,161,051
Chicago	132,419,049	107,047,400
Pacific	78,867,496	69,924,520
American	75,414,298	53,600,442
Philadelphia	49,590,642	49,570,358
Boston	48,711,942	39,221,905
Cincinnati	NA	28,037,238
Montreal	30,330,522	21,063,915
Vancouver	6,781,397	3,571,936
Alberta	2,139,307	980,005
Winnipeg	442	2,348

Annual Volume (in Thousands)		
Exchange	**1993**	**1992**
New York	66,923,276	51,375,671
Toronto	14,882,184	7,326,389
Vancouver	5,748,891	3,899,207
American	4,582,013	3,595,789
Chicago	3,437,293	2,971,505
Montreal	2,705,985	1,683,111
Pacific	2,284,484	2,002,210
Alberta	2,227,652	867,961
Cincinnati	1,226,327	1,203,874
Boston	1,224,167	1,033,357
Philadelphia	1,218,839	1,039,597
Winnipeg	30	15

Source: The *Toronto Stock Exchange Review*, April 1994, p. 6.

either through underwriting or a bought deal;[8] the subsequent trading of these stocks takes place in the secondary market. For example, if the Royal Bank issued new equity, the issue would take place in the primary market; investors who bought the new issue would then trade among themselves in the secondary market. An important role of the secondary market is to signal to the company and to investors the value of the company's shares. As we discuss in chapter 4, accurate share valuation is essential for efficient resource allocation. Another important role of the secondary market is to provide liquidity (i.e., make it possible for the holder of securities to sell them as the need arises). Initial issuances of new stocks would be much more difficult without the comfort of knowing that a secondary market were available.

Stewart (1992) decries the fact that the secondary market is much larger than the primary market, concluding that secondary market activity is "just gambling money, chasing bets around the wheel" (p. 17). He would like to see more primary activity, which he considers to be the true source of new wealth. In essence, the complaint boils down to the notion that the value of new stocks is somehow "too low" relative to the rest of the stock market activity. This reasoning fails to understand the complementary roles of the primary and secondary markets: the secondary market is like a pool representing the accumulation of primary issues in the past, while the primary market is like a stream topping up the pool year-by-year. To refute Stewart's claim, we examine the evidence on primary market activity (new issues) for the Toronto Stock Exchange (the measure of equity for which data are most readily available) and compare it with analogous data for the Canadian government and corporate bond markets, to show that the activities of the stock market are not out of line.

Table 3 shows the value of securities outstanding and net new issues of securities for each of these sectors in 1993.

Looking first at the relative sizes of these markets, it is notable that the value of the stocks of Canadian companies listed on the TSE ($432

---

8 See the glossary for an explanation of these terms.

Table 3: Canadian Capital Market Sectoral Characteristics, 1993 (Billions of Dollars)

Sector	Value	Net New Issues
Corporate Bonds	57	7.8
Government Bonds	200	22.1
TSE Stocks	432	11.6

Sources: *Bank of Canada Review*; Spring 1994, table F2, p. S55; table F4, p. S58; and table G6, p. S80; and *Toronto Stock Exchange Review*, April 1994, p. 6.

billion)[9] is larger than the combined value of outstanding Canadian corporate and government bonds. This gives some perspective as to the relative importance of the stock market in providing capital.

Stewart's complaint that primary market activities are too few has little basis. The value of new issues of stocks on the TSE in 1993 reached $11.6 billion, which is about 3 percent of the value of the stock of Canadian companies listed on the exchange (as well as approximately the same as the growth in gross national product). This compares favourably with the value of new issues of corporate and government bonds as a percentage of their outstanding values (14 percent and 11 percent, respectively). Comparable figures for 1992 are 4 percent for TSE stocks, 12 percent for corporate bonds, and 6 percent for government bonds. These data suggest that the level of primary activity on the TSE is not out of line with that of the bond market (its supposedly staid and beneficent competitor for raising capital), or with economic growth. The stock market is as capable of "topping up the pool" as are competing markets. This evidence, along with the long-term record of stock value appreciation, throws considerable doubt on Stewart's characterization of the stock market as some sort of gambling casino.

---

9 The value for TSE stocks in table 3 is for Canadian-based companies only. Including the (mostly American) listed firms gives a total value for TSE stocks of $862 billion.

Role of derivative securities

Derivative securities are the fastest growing and most controversial aspect of financial markets. Derivatives are securities whose value is "derived" from some underlying asset such as currencies, equities, or commodities, or from an indicator such as the interest rate, or from stock market indices. They include options and futures, as well as other exotic products such as interest rate swaps and currency swaps. The use of options and futures is explained below. Appendix 1a details the use of swaps.

Derivatives are even more misunderstood than are common stocks, and indeed are even feared by many. (The cover story in *Fortune* magazine of March 7, 1994 is entitled "The Risk That Won't Go Away: Like alligators in a swamp, derivatives lurk in the global economy. Even the CEOs of companies that use them don't understand them.") Much of this misunderstanding arises from the seemingly complex mathematical models used to value derivatives. The intuition behind these models is actually straightforward: the values of derivative securities change as the values of the underlying securities change. The Black-Scholes option pricing model is the most widely used model; it represents an application to finance of some fundamental principles of physics. Its development is elegantly described in Bernstein (1992b).

In spite of this widespread trepidation, the volume of trade in derivatives is large and growing quickly. It is estimated that the global "notional" value (that is, the face value of the underlying securities) of derivatives in 1994 stood at $16 trillion, with the value in Canada estimated to be in excess of $2 trillion. What the hype overlooks is that derivatives protect people against risk.

Two of the most commonly traded derivatives are options and futures, and their popularity results from their value as risk management tools. Used properly, they provide a tremendous boost to the financial (and hence real) economy; used improperly, they can truly be "alligators in a swamp." It is worthwhile to understand the difference.

Options and futures

Option contracts offer the holder the option to purchase (call option) or sell (put option) a specified number of shares of stock (usually 100 shares) at a specified price (the strike or exercise price) by a specified time (the maturity of the contract). For example, an Alcan November $25 call gives the holder the option to purchase 100 shares of Alcan stock at $25 each at any time up to the third Friday in November. The option would be valuable if Alcan stock were trading above $25, and worthless if Alcan stock were trading below $25. An Alcan November $25 put has the opposite payoff characteristics: it is valuable if the stock is trading below $25 because the holder can sell the stock at $25, but is worthless if the stock is trading above $25.

Futures contracts are the obligation to purchase (long contract) or sell (short contract) a specified quantity of the underlying asset at a specified price by a specified time. For example, the purchaser of a December three-month bankers' acceptance (BA) contract assumes the obligation to buy $1 million in BAs up to the close of trade in December, at a price determined at the time of purchase. The seller of such a contract assumes the obligation to deliver the BAs in the same time frame. Note that, unlike options, futures contracts do not merely expire worthless if price moves in the wrong direction. Futures contracts are an obligation that does not expire. The purchaser of an option can lose no more than the cost of the option, while the purchaser of a futures contract has a much larger loss potential.

Options on common stocks trade on the Toronto, Montreal, and Vancouver stock exchanges (which together own Trans Canada Options, the clearing house for option trades). Futures contracts trade in futures markets, including the Toronto and Montreal Futures Exchanges and the Winnipeg Commodity Exchange. Montreal is the dominant market in Canada for financial futures trading, while Winnipeg is the major commodity exchange.

Derivatives enhance capital formation

Walter Stewart (1992, p. 133) dismisses all trading in derivatives as mere "bets," and asserts (p. 128) that they "have very little to do with raising money." The previously noted article in *Fortune* magazine goes further and predicts that unconstrained trading in derivatives threatens the very existence of financial markets. Enemies of derivatives do not seem to understand how derivatives protect investors against risk. They believe that the transfer of risk accomplished by the use of derivatives "doesn't wipe it away" (*Fortune*, March 7, 1994, p. 41). Somebody has to bear the residual risk, and that risk can be very large. Recent well-documented examples such as the case of Metallgesellschaft's "hedging mismatch" in oil futures confirm this possibility. If derivatives are used properly, however, risk does get "wiped away," and derivatives do have an important economic role.

Both options and futures provide investors with the opportunity to hedge a position in the underlying security (i.e., to reduce or eliminate risk, for example by making it possible for the investor to sell the security at some future time at a price agreed in advance, regardless of what happens to the actual market price) or to speculate on price movements. This facility enhances the liquidity of secondary trading and enables the investor or the company to offset risk. Investors do not like risk. Derivatives provide investors with a way to fine tune how much risk they will bear. Risk reduction is accomplished through the hedging feature of derivatives illustrated below. Liquidity is enhanced because of the comfort provided by the risk-reduction mechanism. Investors will be wary of investing if the risk level is too high for their taste. On the other hand, they will be more likely to trade if they can reduce their risk exposure, and markets consequently will be more liquid. More liquidity means that more money is available for capital formation and economic development. Both the liquidity and risk-reducing attributes of derivative securities contribute to the breadth of the market (number of participants) and hence have a good deal to do with "raising money."

Hedging of risk

"Hedging," in the world of finance, means protecting yourself against some risk in case things go badly. The stock market has developed financial instruments that allow investors to hedge, or, in other words, to buy insurance, for almost any kind of risky venture.

Figure 1: Call Option—Payoff Profile

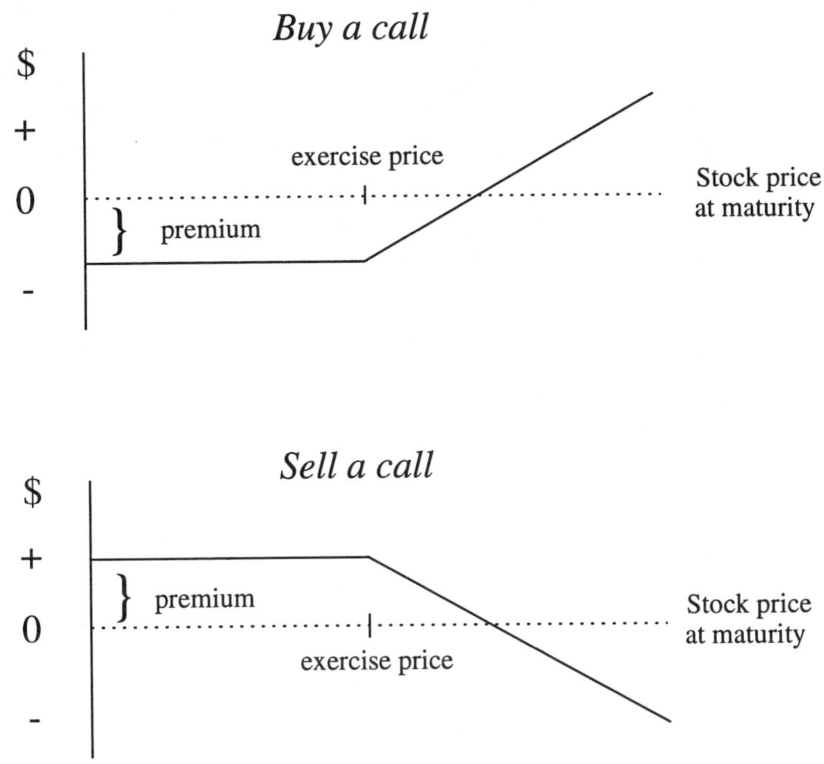

Two examples will illustrate how hedging of risk works.[10] Figure 1 shows the payoff profiles from buying or selling a call option. Remember that a call option gives you the choice to buy a stock at a specified price and that this choice lasts only for a specified period of time. An investor who thinks the stock price is going to go up beyond the price specified at the time of purchase (the exercise price) would purchase a

10 The examples that follow are illustrative only. For a complete description of the roles of derivative securities, see Cox and Rubinstein (1985).

call option and later, if the stock price goes up, as he or she foresaw, he or she would have the right to buy the stock at the low exercise price. If the price does go up above the exercise price, the investor makes a profit equal to the excess of the actual price over the exercise price. This profit is, of course, reduced by the amount paid for the option, i.e., the "premium." Who would sell a call option? Somebody who believes the price will not rise above the exercise price would. The receipts from the sale of the option (the premium) represent the profit.

Figure 2 shows the payoff profiles from buying or selling a put option. The investor expecting the stock price to drop below the exercise

Figure 2: Put Option—Payoff Profile

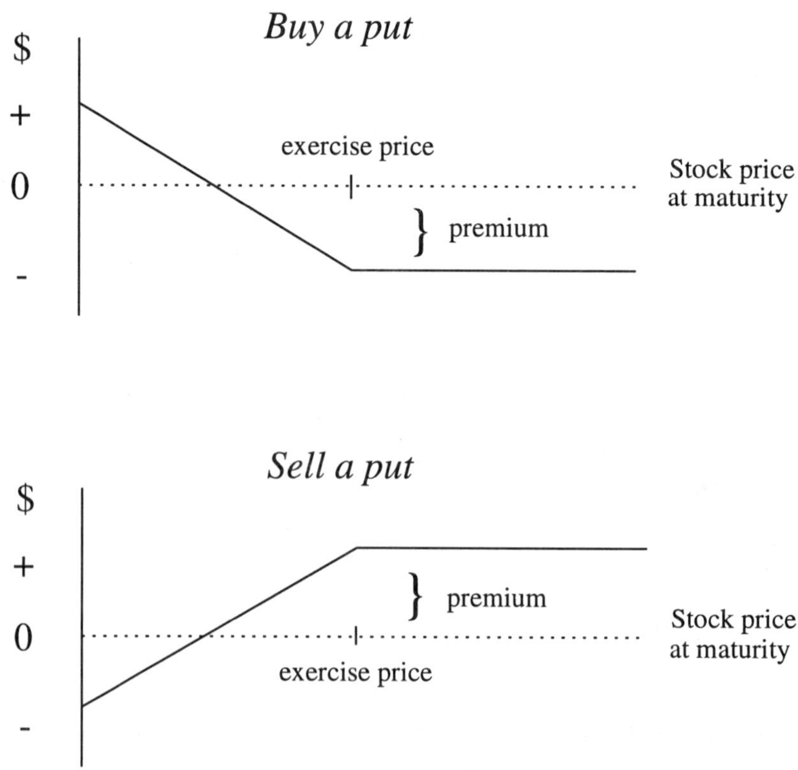

price can purchase a put option and sell ("put") the stock at the exercise price if the stock price does indeed decline. Conversely, the investor who does not expect the stock price to decline, or expects an increase, would sell the put option.

How do these instruments improve the market? Consider as an example an investor whose stock has increased in value, and who does not want to lose the gains made to date. For example, this could be a pensioner who is very concerned with the security of capital. He or she has two choices: sell the stock and leave the market, or buy a put option with an exercise price equal to the current stock price. If the stock price does decline, the put is exercised, allowing the holder of the put to sell the stock at the exercise price, not at the now lower actual stock price, and the value of the stock is locked in (less the cost of the option). If the stock price does not decline, the put expires worthless. The put option in this instance has acted as a form of insurance; its existence has stabilized the underlying stock market since otherwise the stock would have been sold, causing price pressure and a drop in liquidity, since the investor would have left the market. This feature is particularly attractive when markets are volatile, as it defers some price pressure during turbulent periods.

The combination of a stock position and a put option just described is known as a "protective put" strategy. There is a wide variety of option-based strategies involving combinations of stocks with options or options with options (see Cox and Rubinstein 1985, for a more detailed discussion). All of these strategies are forms of insurance, in that they offer investors the opportunity to minimize risk at a small cost. Their existence benefits the market by stabilizing prices and allaying investors' natural aversion to risk. This means that more people are willing to invest so the result is more capital and more investment, hence more economic growth.

This function is analogous to any form of insurance. Consumers routinely purchase such insurance for their homes, automobiles, and lives, and the proper use of derivatives can be thought of in the same mundane manner. Consumers do not routinely buy car or home insurance from each other. However, in the stock market, some investors sell call or put options and others buy them—in other words, people trade

Figure 3: Hedging with Futures Contracts—Wheat Futures		
September delivery	**April**	**September**
Farmer	Sells Futures @ 100	Buys Futures or Delivers
Miller	Buys Futures @ 100	Sells Futures or Accepts Delivery

in a "commodity" called risk. Those who are less tolerant of risk will pay for security, and others who are better informed or better prepared to absorb punishment will sell security, i.e., willingly burden themselves with extra risk. Stock markets thus provide a valuable service to the process of economic growth by developing and trading derivatives and other instruments for reallocating risks among consumers according to their risk preferences.

Futures markets provide a similar insurance function. Figures 3 and 4 demonstrate the economic role of contracts in wheat futures. We have chosen wheat futures for this example because they are more intuitively understandable: the same principles apply to financial futures such as those in treasury bills, bankers' acceptances, or stock indexes.

Figure 3 shows the actions of a wheat farmer and a miller before and after the crop has been harvested. The wheat farmer would like some guarantee of the price at which the crop can be sold; similarly, the miller would like some guarantee of the costs of raw materials. The farmer is insuring against a price decline, and the miller is insuring against a price increase.

In this example, the farmer sells the expected crop to the miller in April, for delivery in September, at a price of $100 a tonne. This is a futures contract representing an obligation for delivery in the future at a price specified in advance. In September, the farmer delivers it to the miller, and the miller accepts delivery, paying the farmer $100 per tonne. We assume here that the size of the crop and the miller's actual requirements in September turn out to be what was expected in April. If this were not the case, the farmer or the miller would have to buy or sell sufficient futures contracts to balance the position.

Figure 4: Hedging With Futures Contracts—Payoffs

Farmer			
September Wheat Price	**Futures Position**	**Spot Position**	**Total**
90	+ 10	90	100
100	0	100	100
110	- 10	110	100
Miller			
September Wheat Price	**Futures Position**	**Spot Position**	**Total**
90	- 10	- 90	- 100
100	0	- 100	- 100
110	+ 10	- 110	- 100

Figure 4 summarizes the financial positions of the farmer and the miller in September, for three possible price levels of wheat: $90, $100, or $110 per tonne (these are called "spot" prices, as they represent the price of the commodity on the spot, as opposed to at some future date). If the spot price of wheat in September is only $90, the farmer still receives $100 income per tonne for the wheat, as agreed upon in April. In effect, the farmer receives $90 per tonne on the wheat and $10 per tonne on the futures position, i.e., the futures contract is $10 "in the money." The miller's costs are $100 for the wheat accepted for delivery and consist of paying $90 per tonne for the wheat and losing $10 per tonne on the futures contract, since the miller had agreed to buy wheat for $100 that is now selling for only $90.

The farmer and the miller are both happy with this arrangement. The miller "lost" $10 on the futures position in this scenario but was able to guarantee raw material costs. To make this clear, suppose wheat sells at $110 per tonne in September. The farmer has "lost" $10 on the futures position in this case (since spot wheat is now $110 but the crop has been sold for $100), but was able to achieve the expected income from the crop. In both cases, the futures contract has acted as a form of insurance guaranteeing the price of wheat agreed upon in April. Such guarantees reduce the risk of doing business for both sides of the transaction.

Similar activities take place in many other markets. For instance, bond investors concerned with adverse movements in interest rates can insure their holdings with bond futures. The prices of bonds move in the opposite direction to the level of interest rates; if rates move up, bond prices fall. Bond futures allow investors to protect themselves against such occurrences. Gold producers can lock in a guaranteed price for their lode using gold futures. (American Barrick is an excellent example of this activity, having sold much of its output in the futures market for $400 plus an ounce at a time when spot prices languished around $375.) Companies with international activities can hedge against adverse foreign exchange movements using currency futures, thus enhancing international trade. These transactions, contrary to popular opinion, are not inherently risky. In fact, it can be argued that investors and companies who do not hedge in circumstances such as those above are the ones taking on unnecessary risk.

Speculation

Situations in which an agent has both a futures contract and a position in the underlying commodity, as in the case of the farmer and the miller, are called "hedged" positions. They stabilize the market and reduce risk in the same manner as do options. Situations in which the agent does not have an offsetting position in the underlying commodity are known as "speculative" positions. The presence of speculators in the market provides liquidity and helps to ensure that futures prices are stable and not out of line with spot prices.

For example, in the wheat example above, it is highly unlikely that exactly the same amount of wheat would be demanded by millers (and other processors) and supplied by farmers. Speculators balance supply and demand by providing liquidity, i.e., they gravitate to the market when supply-demand imbalances affect prices, and their trading tends to even out these imbalances. Similarly, their actions help to ensure that prices of different contracts are consistent. If, for example, the prices of wheat for December and January delivery differed too much, speculators would buy the cheaper contract and sell the dearer one until consistency in prices were attained. In other words, speculators move resources from where they are less likely to be valued to where they are more likely to be valued. This helps to stabilize prices both in the futures market and in the spot market.

The effect of derivative securities on the underlying stock market

There are conflicting views on the effect of the burgeoning trade in derivative securities on the underlying stock markets. The advocates of derivative securities argue, as we have done above, that their existence provides additional hedging opportunities for stock investors, and thus adds to liquidity and helps spread risk. The detractors see derivatives not as complements, but as substitutes for stocks—investors have the opportunity to replicate any stock portfolio with derivatives without incurring transactions costs, and can do so largely outside the existing regulatory system.[11] These so-called "synthetic securities" have experienced considerable growth but their aggregate use still pales when compared to stock-market-related derivative activity. It is therefore hard to believe that unregulated trading in derivatives represents any serious competitive threat to Canadian stock markets.

Another widespread but unfounded belief is that trading in derivative markets makes stock trading more volatile. For example, the stock market crash of October 1987 has been blamed by some on arbitrage traders operating in both stock and derivative markets.[12] Arbitrage involves simultaneously buying and selling the same good (or its equivalent) for a certain profit. An example is an investor with two telephones, connected to gold trading desks in London and New York. If the price of gold in New York is $390 an ounce and in London is $400

---

11 See, for example, Grundfest (1993). Stoll (1993) examines this phenomenon for derivative markets as well as for other alternative outlets, such as NASDAQ and foreign markets.

12 For a detailed analysis of the 1987 crash from the perspective of the NYSE, see Reilly (1989, pp. 120-149). More succinct summaries of the event focused on the TSE are provided by Hatch and Robinson (1989, pp. 399-403) and Hatch and White (1989, pp. 17-22).

an ounce, the investor simultaneously buys in New York (at $390) and sells in London (at $400), guaranteeing a profit of $10 an ounce. These arbitrage activities ensure that prices for the same good in different markets are the same. In the stock and derivative markets, arbitrage normally takes the form of "program trading," where prices in both markets are tracked electronically and a computer is programmed to trigger a trade whenever a profitable arbitrage opportunity presents itself.

The allegation that derivative trading adds to stock market volatility has not been confirmed by real world evidence. Bernstein (1992b) reviews academic studies that examine market volatility dating back to 1802 and concludes that volatility has not varied much over the two centuries (except for the 1928-1937 period). He believes that researchers are "unanimous in agreeing that the events of October 1987 [the market crash] were an anomaly" (p. 304), and notes that futures markets were closed by regulators during the subsequent October 1989 market collapse, and hence could not have affected stock market prices or volatility. Chamberlain, Cheung, and Kwan (1993) show that the listing of options on Canadian stocks has no effect on the volatility of returns or trading volume. No evidence has been presented to date to support the alleged volatility-inducing role of derivatives.

Debate about the potential destabilizing effects of derivatives peaked in mid-1994, when the U.S. General Accounting Office, the investigative arm of Congress, called for increasing regulation of over-the-counter (OTC) derivatives markets. The GAO feared that derivative trading would precipitate a financial emergency in the system requiring another federal bail-out of banks. (Note that the GAO's concerns relate to OTC derivatives and not to the exchange-traded products).

The response to the GAO's initiatives has been rapid, with most parties decrying increased regulation. Among the reactions, Nicholas Close of the Bank of Canada called for more disclosure and increased transparency rather than increased regulation.[13] Finance Minister Paul Martin welcomed the introduction of new TSE-based options by saying: "Properly used, derivatives are an important tool for investors and

---

13 The *Financial Post*, May 20, 1994, p. 6.

financial institutions to manage and reduce risks. They are a sign of highly developed competitive capital markets."[14] Other observers, including Alan Greenspan, Chairman of the Federal Reserve Board, noted that the imposition of increased regulation could have a negative effect by discouraging companies and institutions from using derivatives to reduce risk.[15] Contemporaneous draft guidelines issued for Canada by the Office of the Superintendent of Financial Institutions recognize many of the risks discussed here and emphasize the need for further disclosure of derivative trading activity.

A series of articles in *The Economist* (May 14-20, 1994) repeated this theme, calling for increased disclosure rather than increased regulation. For instance:

> Vigilance is reassuring; ill-conceived legislation is not. Laws that stifled the growth of derivatives could actually increase systemic risk, by restricting the ability of companies to manage their risk by hedging (insuring themselves) against adverse price movements in volatile markets. Derivatives have other benefits too. They encourage economic efficiency by signalling to producers and consumers the likely future prices of commodities. And by helping to cut the cost of mortgages and student loans, they benefit Main Street, not just Wall Street.[16]

In a later article in the same issue, it was noted that much of the fear surrounding derivatives results from their being largely misunderstood. The article concludes that markets are much better assessors of risk than are governments, and the complexity of derivatives by itself is not sufficient reason for increased regulation. A nice analogy is given to motor cars—their innards are sometimes complicated, but that is no reason to argue for more traffic lights.[17]

---

14 The *Globe and Mail*, May 18, 1994, p. B11.

15 The *Financial Post*, May 18, 1994, P. 9; The *Globe and Mail*, May 26, 1994, p. B8.

16 The *Economist*, May 14-20, 1994, p. 15.

17 *Ibid.*, p. 24.

Functions of stock markets

Stock markets are more than a convenient place to trade securities. Their development has fostered economic growth by providing a link between savers and users of capital, and by assisting investors in spreading risks through diversification.

Pooling of funds

To illustrate the first function, consider Canada in the absence of a central market, with individual investors located in St. John's, Moncton, Val d'Or, Moose Jaw, and Yellowknife. An investor wishing to buy or sell a stock would be obliged to call every other investor in the loop to ensure that he or she was getting the most favourable price. Figure 5 shows the network of communication channels required for these five investors. In the absence of a central market, ten individual channels are needed to complete the loop.[18]

Now add a central market, for example in Toronto. It is clear from figure 6 that the number of required channels is reduced to five (n, the number of investors). This efficiency gain is magnified when one considers much larger numbers of investors and the geographic dispersion of the Canadian population. This effect is known as operational (or transactional) efficiency of the market, and is discussed in more detail in chapter 4.

Financial markets with central locations do more than simplify the logistics of transacting among different agents. They also facilitate the pooling of resources, so that issuers of equity or debt need not seek out—on their own—large numbers of individual investors or lenders. Consider a Canadian company, say a steel company, which wants to raise new equity to finance an expansion of its plant. Now consider a number of individual Canadian investors who are separately looking for investment opportunities in the industrial sector. The stock market provides a mechanism (the new issue market) for investors to pool their

---

18 In general, the requirement for n investors is $(n(n-1))/2$ channels. (In this example, $n = 5$, and the number of channels is $(5)(4)/2 = 10$.)

Figure 5: Canada--No Central Market

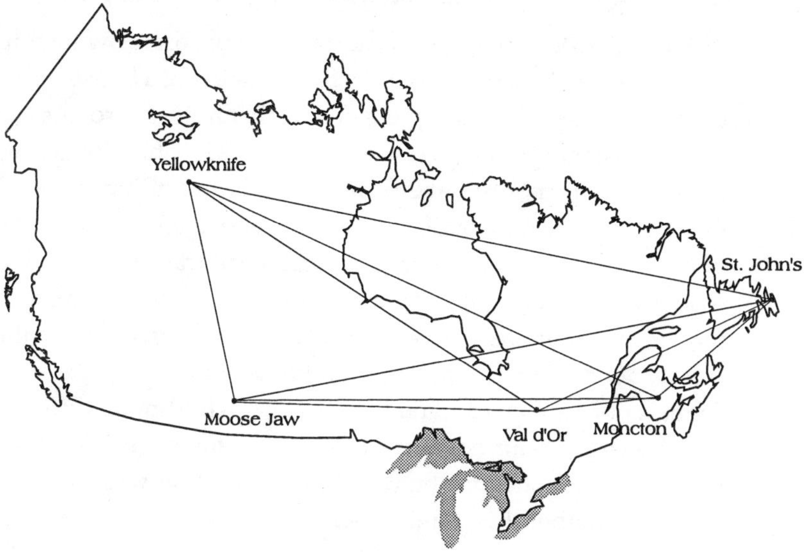

Figure 6: Canada--Central Market

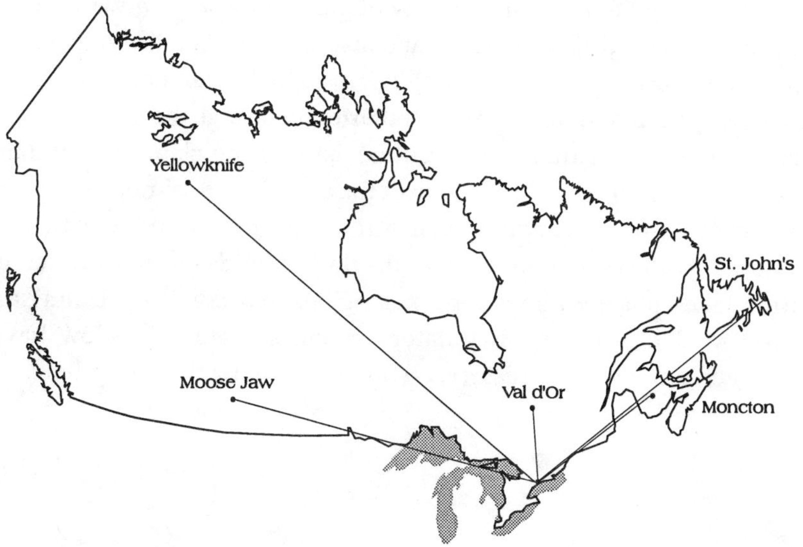

individual resources, and the steel company can access this pool directly.

Bernstein (1992b, p. 299) suggests a nice analogy for this role:

> Without the stock market, the market for corporate ownership would be like the market for houses. The seller of a house offers the entire house, not just a piece of it. Only rarely do brokers use their own capital to buy a house for resale. They have to advertise or resort to more cumbersome methods for finding the other side of the deal; no wonder the realtors earn a commission of 6 percent (the commission on a typical stock transaction is less than 1 percent), and no wonder transactions involve such extended negotiations. After the house has been sold, only the principals and their close friends know what the price was. Transactions are few and far between. With trading so difficult, so expensive, so infrequent, and so secret, the buyer and seller seldom know whether the price they settled on was the right price or whether they might not have struck a better deal with someone else.

Similar pooling services are also provided by the other three "pillars" of the financial intermediation industry (banks, trusts, and insurance companies).

Figure 7 gives a schematic view of the relationship between financial intermediaries (banks, trusts, and insurance companies) and market intermediaries (brokerage houses). The principal difference between the two groups is that financial intermediaries repackage the funds (deposits, trust funds, insurance premiums), so that the claims of ultimate creditors are indirect. In other words, the consumer does not see the link between his or her deposit or insurance premium and a loan to a commercial developer. In contrast, the flow of funds through brokerage firms takes place without repackaging, so that creditors' claims are direct, and transparent. Regulatory changes discussed below have, however, blurred these historic distinctions among the four pillars.

Figure 7: Canadian Intermediation System

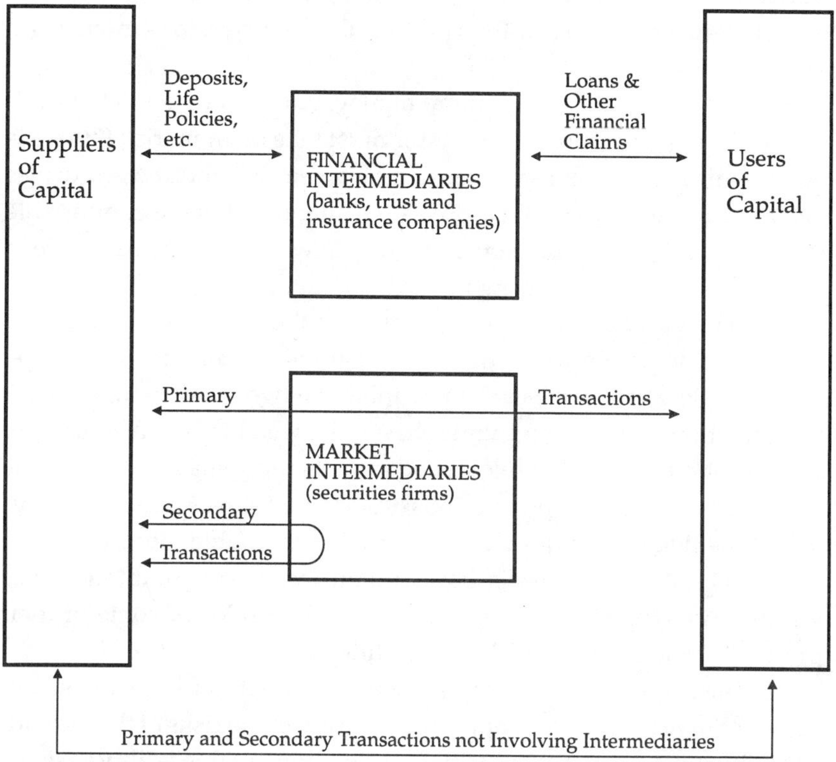

Source: See footnote 12.

From "Regulation and Ownership of Market Intermediaries in Canada," *Report of the Joint Securities Industry Committee on behalf of the Alberta, Montreal, Toronto, and Vancouver Stock Exchanges and the Investment Dealers Association of Canada,* September 19, 1984.

Spreading of risks

One of the most important functions performed by all intermediaries, including the stock market, is the spreading of risks. The pooling activity described above does more than accumulate sums of money; it permits participants to spread investment risk through diversification. For example, a bank deposit may be transformed into (parts of) several automobile loans. This is not as risky as making a single loan on a single lender's own account. Similarly, investing in a mutual fund or in a basket of stocks is less risky than putting all of the investor's money into a single stock.

Investors naturally want more money, but it is an inevitable truth that to get higher returns the investor must take on more risk ("there is no free lunch"). The constant tension between risk and reward drives much stock market activity, as investors attempt to find a comfortable mix of the two. Diversification is one way in which investors are able to reduce risk while maximizing reward.

The magic of diversification is based on the observable fact that all companies do not perform equally as economic circumstances change. For example, at a resort beach there might be two vendors, one selling suntan lotion and the other umbrellas. If the weather is sunny, sales of suntan lotion are brisk while nobody wants umbrellas; if it rains, the opposite is the case. During periods of sustained sun or rain conditions, one of the two businesses would be in serious trouble. But, consider a "conglomerate" which sells both suntan lotion and umbrellas. The weather no longer matters, since there will be sales of some of their products under any atmospheric condition.

In the same way, diversifying across a variety of common stocks provides investors with an opportunity to offset the risks of the individual companies against each other. Investors can use this facility to shape the amount of risk they are willing to bear, either through selecting their own mixes of securities, or through investing in mutual funds. Mutual funds very carefully outline their expected income and risk profiles so that investors can match the appropriate funds with their degrees of risk tolerance. The stock market thus provides a vital social function because it allows people to adjust their expected future consumption streams (and their riskiness) as they see fit. Interestingly, this is a function usually ascribed to welfare states; here the stock market implicitly does the work of government without its accompanying bureaucracy.

Current and future trends

Stock markets as we know them now are much different than those of even a decade ago. Traditionally, industry sales people (called variously stock brokers, registered representatives, or investment executives) charged a fixed rate of commission for buying and selling stocks on behalf of clients. This fixed rate covered not only the broker's compensation but also contributed to the overhead of the brokerage firm, including the in-house economics and research departments. The broker provided the client with investment advice, and also provided access to in-house economic forecasts and research reports. These non-transaction services are called "soft dollar services," and the investor had no choice but to pay for them, regardless of whether he or she wanted them.

Deregulation in Canada of commissions and unbundling of soft dollar services following the "Little Bang" of 1987[19] opened up opportunities for discount brokers and resulted in a segmented market comprising, on the one hand, large full service firms and, on the other, small boutique firms, while essentially eliminating mid-size brokerage houses. Changes in financial regulations allowing banks to own brokerage houses have led to a further reduction in the number of existing firms, as global competition calls for larger pools of capital.

The exchanges themselves have changed dramatically. Floor trading is rapidly becoming obsolete, and computer systems such as Toronto's CATS (Computer Assisted Trading System) are gradually displacing the traditional open outcry system.[20] The development of competing markets (OTC, institutional off-floor trading, interlisted

---

19 The "Big Bang" took place in London in 1986, a massive deregulation which eliminated fixed commission rates and allowed freer access to the London exchange by foreign brokerage firms. Soft dollar services are those not related to the actual trading of securities; they include research reports, economists' briefings, seminars, and travel.

20 Kirzner (1992) discusses the pros (the enhancement of "fairness, visibility, and accessibility") and the cons (dealing with priority rules for competing bid and ask prices, determining the role of market makers, and reducing downtime from computer malfunctions) of the "new electronic world."

stocks) and competing instruments (derivative securities) threatens the livelihood of the traditional exchanges, which depend on transaction fee income for their viability. Competition among exchanges has intensified as markets move to a 24-hour trading day. Interest groups periodically call for reform and re-regulation of stock markets to control the alleged rampant miscreant behaviour.

The speed of this change is remarkable. As recently as 1980, a contemporary commentary on the stock market included the following observation:

> Without the floor, there would be no Exchange—no administration, no upstairs members, no subsidiary organizations, and no satellite companies that exist in the Wall Street area because, like Mount Everest, the floor is there. The main function of the Exchange is to serve as an auction medium for trading securities, and the floor is the place where the trading is done. Although detractors talk, sometimes wistfully, sometimes antagonistically, about an electronic "black box" in New Jersey or Cincinnati replacing the entire apparatus of the New York exchange, the floor seems likely to continue to function in one shape or another for many years to come. (Sloane, 1980, p. 5)

The transition has not been entirely painless. Floor traders in Toronto have fought the move to electronic trading for several years, and violence occurred in Paris when the Bourse went to electronic trading (using the TSE's CATS technology). Computer systems have also failed completely on occasion, and these experiences have delayed the transition to all-electronic trading in many exchanges, including the TSE. Change is inevitable, however, and markets must continue to adapt if they are to survive.

Some problematic features of stock markets

Stock markets are often criticized for having a large-firm bias: established firms have access to stock markets, while new ventures typically do not.[21] However, as the economy restructures and rationalizes in the face of a lingering recession and the consequences of freer trade agreements, it is the small and medium-sized business that provides much of the growth. The relevance of existing stock markets is therefore challenged by these developments, especially as venture capital firms become more established as an alternative source of capital.[22] The development of a two-tier market (proposed in chapter 7) would provide more scope for many of these junior firms.

There is also a potential cause for concern about the sectoral characteristics of companies whose stocks still dominate trading on stock markets. Economist Nuala Beck (1992) has studied the restructuring of the economy, and has identified two groups of industries. One consists of the new growth sectors—the New Economy, led by computers, instrumentation, health care, and telecommunications. The other represents the old, allegedly decaying sectors—the Old Economy, including tobacco, steel, integrated oils, and breweries. Her analysis of the TSE 300 concludes that the New Economy stocks comprise only 39 percent, while the Old Economy stocks still represent 56 percent of trading (the remaining stocks being on what she calls the watch list).[23]

The concern here, in Beck's terms, is that economies should be investing in areas likely to be at the centre of global economic activity in the future. The preponderance of Old Economy stocks supposedly dilutes the available investment pool and misdirects investment dollars that could be better spent on New Economy investments. Beck's critique might be stronger if in fact it were true that Old Economy industries were stagnant. Contrary to fashionable opinion, though, many of these

---

21 Stock markets are not alone in this bias. A recent study based on data from the Canadian Federation of Independent Business shows that banks provide less credit and on harsher terms to small companies than to larger companies. The study is reported in the Globe and Mail Report on Business, July 13, 1993, p. B4.

22 See Fletcher (1992) for a discussion of the Canadian venture capital industry.

23 Data as of July 1993. Source: The *Globe and Mail*, July 6, 1993, p. B18.

supposedly dying industries have recently revived as they have adapted to the needs for high technology and low costs.

The stock market must be alert to several other factors that potentially threaten its importance: increasingly global markets (capital knows no borders, so domestic loyalty cannot be guaranteed), innovations in financial instruments (which can replicate stock returns but which do not trade on stock exchanges), and the proliferation of electronic trading systems (which can compete for stock transaction business without bearing the heavy overhead of physical exchanges).

Kirzner (1990, 41) identifies nine fundamental changes, which are:

> raising the pressure for reform [by government] of Canada's equity markets [requiring]: (1) the abolition of fixed commission rates; (2) increasing transactions volume; (3) expanding over-the-counter markets; (4) institutional trading dominance; (5) periodic bouts of extreme volatility; (6) the introduction of derivatives markets which must interact with the cash markets; (7) major realignments within the traditionally segmented financial services industry; (8) market globalization and round the clock trading; [and] (9) movement towards international regulatory and security clearance systems.

Reform is always a contentious issue, and many advocates of reform may have hidden agendas. Chapter 4 shows that Canadian markets are reasonably efficient, which should allay many of Kirzner's concerns. Chapter 7 deals with the need for reform directly, and concludes that misguided regulation is not the answer for Canada's stock markets.

Summary

The continuing prosperity of an economy depends on well-functioning stock markets. They provide a market-place for risk capital and a vehicle for risk management by investors. Stock market activity ensures an adequate supply of capital for economic development by satisfying both the corporate need for capital and the investor need for flexibility and security. Many developments in stock markets, such as the creation of new types of financial instruments, are truly innovative, and have worked to the good of the small investor.

To many, the stock market is a mystery, if not a sinister being. We have tried to uncloak some of that mystery in this chapter, and to debunk some of the myths surrounding its activity. The evolving structure of stock markets along with some of the new financial innovations have transformed the market for capital. There are advantages resulting from the proper use of derivative securities, and their alleged role in destabilizing the financial system has not been shown. As well, the market's central functions serve to satisfy the investor's need to pool funds and to spread risks. In the next chapter we turn to the role of the stock market in shaping the way in which corporations are run.

Appendix 1a: Currency Swaps and Interest Rate Swaps

SWAPS ARE DERIVATIVE SECURITIES in which two entities (called by convention the "party" and the "counterparty") each take out a loan in a market in which they have preferred access and then swap to the market in which they want to be. The concept is best understood through example, which we undertake here for the two major types of swaps, currency swaps and interest rate swaps. The examples are simplified but capture the essence of the transactions.

Currency swaps

Northern Telecom is a Canadian company, which, we will assume, plans to open a plant in France. Its operating income will be in francs, so the company faces exposure to foreign exchange risk (i.e., the risk that the franc depreciates against the Canadian dollar). It would like to have its expenses denominated in francs so as to reduce this exposure. This is called an "operating hedge." Consequently, Northern Telecom would like to borrow the money for the plant in francs rather than in dollars.

EDF Industrie is a French company, which, we will assume, plans to open a plant in Canada. Its operating income will be in dollars, and it faces currency risk opposite to that of Northern Telecom, i.e., its risk is that the dollar depreciates against the franc. Consequently, EDF would like to borrow the money for its plant in Canadian dollars to hedge its operating income.

Northern Telecom, then, wants to borrow in France, while EDF wants to borrow in Canada. Northern Telecom, however, is better known in Canada than in France, and could borrow more easily and on better terms in Canada than in France. In the same way, EDF has preferred access to the French market.

The solution to this dilemma is as follows. Northern Telecom borrows in Canada and EDF borrows a similar amount in France. The two companies then swap their debt obligations, with Northern Telecom assuming the interest payments denominated in francs and EDF assuming the interest payments denominated in Canadian dollars. Both companies are better off then if they had borrowed directly in the currency of choice.

Interest rate swaps

Northern Telecom also wants to borrow (we will assume) some money in Canada to finance its domestic operations. It wants to borrow at a floating rate, which would cost it seven percent, but it could also borrow at a fixed rate of eight percent. With the floating rate loan, as the name suggests, the interest rate fluctuates over time, but with the fixed rate loan it does not.

Meanwhile, Boondock Mining wants to borrow at a fixed rate, which would cost it 16 percent, but it could also borrow at a floating rate of 11 percent. Notice that the fixed rate market has a risk premium of eight percentage points (16 percent for Boondock versus 8 percent for Northern Telecom) because of Boondock's higher risk, while the floating rate market has a risk premium of only four percentage points (11 percent versus 7 percent). These spreads are common, as the fixed rate market tends to differentiate more on credit risk than does the floating rate market. Northern Telecom in this example has preferred access to the fixed rate market.

To summarize, Northern Telecom wants a floating rate loan, which would cost seven percent, while Boondock Mining wants a fixed rate loan, which would cost it 16 percent. Both companies can do better by arranging a swap, as follows. Northern Telecom borrows in the fixed rate market (at eight percent), while Boondock borrows at the floating rate of 11 percent. They then swap the loans to arrive in their preferred markets.

Boondock is obviously well ahead of the game at this point, nominally paying a fixed rate of eight percent instead of the 16 percent it would pay if it borrowed on its own. Northern Telecom appears to be the loser, paying a nominal rate of 11 percent versus the seven percent it would pay on its own. However, if Boondock pays to Northern Telecom annually the equivalent of six percent of the loan, Boondock's effective cost of the loan becomes 14 percent (eight plus six), while Northern Telecom's effective cost becomes five percent (eleven minus six). Both companies have reduced their effective rates by two percentage points (14 percent versus 16 percent for Boondock and 5 percent versus 7 percent for Northern Telecom).

Chapter 2: The Role of the Stock Market in Corporate Governance

Introduction

THE STOCK MARKET ACTS AS THE NEXUS OR LINK between the owners of a company and its managers. The stock market assists owners (shareholders) in disciplining managers, for it is through the market that shareholders can vote their pleasure or displeasure about management's actions through the sale and purchase of the company's stocks. In the next two chapters we examine several aspects of the stock market's role in corporate governance as one of the social benefits of this particular mechanism for allocation of resources.

Holders of common stocks, unlike those of other financial assets, are the owners of the company, and the trading of stocks allocates the ownership of companies listed on the stock exchange. This chapter focuses on two aspects of ownership with particular reference to Canadian stock markets: the separation of ownership and control, and differential voting shares. Corporate takeovers, through which the "market for corporate control" disciplines managers who ignore shareholder interests, are discussed in chapter 3.

The separation of ownership and control in a company can lead to agency problems. That is, the manager acts as the agent for the owners and may pursue self-serving behaviour at the expense of the shareholders. The board of directors is supposed to act as a monitor of management, but there are areas of weakness in this role. The stock market provides a means of controlling these problems. It has also been alleged (by Porter, among others) that institutional shareholders have a short-term performance focus that tends to force management into myopic decision-making. We conclude that Canadian firms are no worse in this regard than are American firms, but they may be at a competitive disadvantage relative to Japanese and European competitors.

An area of increasing controversy is differential voting shares—different classes of shares for a company may have a different number of votes. We outline some of the dangers of concentrated ownership that result from different votes for some shares, and explain why institutional investors have been recently more aggressive in demanding shareholder democracy.

Separation of ownership and control

Modern corporations are, with notable exceptions, too large and too complex to be owned and managed by a single owner or family group.[24] Inevitably, the professional manager has emerged—a corporate executive who, although very capable, may have goals and objectives other than maximizing the value of the owners' investment. The managers report, through the board of directors, to the company's owners, the stockholders, who (at least in principle) have the final say.[25]

---

24 This is less the case in Canada than in the U.S., but even here the legacy of legendary corporate pioneers and entrepreneurs is becoming dissipated as new generations are often not able to or interested in carrying on the family business. Occasional intra-family battles such as those of the Billes and McCain families also threaten the continuity of family ownership.

25 There is a large literature (known as agency theory) on the problem of how owners can control management behaviour, the seminal work being that of Jensen and Meckling (1976). Our treatment differs from their approach: while, in general, agency theory assumes that the goals of the firm and the

The board of directors is the main instrument of shareholder control over management decisions, even though its effectiveness is questionable, since managers typically control the selection of directors. The directors who are insiders are usually loyal to management, and those who are outsiders frequently have a financial interest in the continuity of management (e.g., directors who are lawyers or advertisers for the firm). Similarly, handling management succession is typically the prerogative of the departing chief executive officer (Shleifer and Vishny, 1988, pp. 8-9).

Boards of directors are at a disadvantage (as compared to management) in fulfilling their mandates of governance. Their main limitation is the insufficient amount of information they possess, especially with respect to decisions as to which lines of business the firm should enter or exit.

The ability of a CEO to pursue non-value-maximizing behaviour is enhanced by the lack of effectiveness of the boards, as well as by the "business judgment" rule, which limits the power of courts to interfere in the affairs of corporations.[26] When internal incentives and other devices for disciplining managers fail, the stock market may have to come to the rescue: hostile takeovers are an alternative mechanism for replacing non-value-maximizing managers (as we discuss in chapter 3).

Several recent corporate failures have heated up the debate as to whether boards of directors, and particularly independent directors, have been exercising sufficient diligence over management activities.[27] In 1993, the Toronto Stock Exchange established a Committee on Corporate Governance in Canada to study and make recommendations to improve Canadian corporate governance. The committee, under the chairmanship of Peter Dey, reported in May 1994. Its recommendations

---

owners are congruent, we see them as possibly being in conflict.

26 The Canadian common law doctrine that guides courts in this area derives from the English case *Re City Equitable Fire Insurance Company Limited* [1925]1, ch. 407.

27 For an interesting discussion of the case of Royal Trustco, see the *Globe and Mail's* "Report on Business," July 19, 1993, pp. B1 and B3.

relate to the need for more independence for outside board members. TSE president Pearce Bunting commented on the report as follows: "The Exchange believes that good governance plays a vital role in promoting investor confidence in our capital markets."[28] This need for investor confidence is an important theme, which we encounter frequently in this book. As we will see in this chapter, the stock market is capable of dealing with these problems.

Institutional investors

Some concerns

Institutional investors are financial institutions, such as pension plans, insurance companies, and mutual funds, that invest money on behalf of others. For Porter (1992), "transient" institutional investors who seek near-term results as reflected in quarterly financial reports are the key reason for the divergence of interest between owners and managers. This short-term focus pressures managers to make myopic (short-sighted) investments instead of more far-sighted, longer-term investments. Porter contrasts this "fluid capital" behaviour (i.e., capital with no loyalty, that can be moved quickly from one company to another) with the Japanese and German concept of "dedicated capital" (i.e., capital that is invested for the long term). He claims that the fluid capital myopia hampers longer-term investment planning, particularly in intangible investments such as human capital and research and development (R&D). In a global, technologically driven economy, the ultimate consequences of failure to invest in knowledge and R&D are dim; hence, the story goes, the alleged shortsightedness of North American stock markets has contributed to the current dominance of Asian and European companies in world trade.

There are three other complaints about institutional stock ownership. Institutional stock owners come under fire for their purported "herd" mentality. Since few fund managers want to appear to be different from the rest, individual stocks or sectors of stocks move in or out

---

28 The *Globe and Mail*, May 17, 1994, p. B1.

of favour with most of them at the same time, and large price swings result. It is also alleged that smaller, and especially newer, companies find it difficult to attract institutional interest. This is partly because many institutions are legally bound to invest in older, more established companies. As well, the liquidity needs of the institutions are also important. They have large capital bases and tend to trade stocks in large blocks; when the company in question is small, its stock price may be drastically affected by large trades. Finally, institutions may have preferential access to new stock issues, for example through private placements (which can only be marketed to "sophisticated investors").[29]

The evidence on institutional ownership

In spite of some of these complaints, institutional ownership is a positive force for the stock market. The sheer size of institutional owners serves to ensure that they are able to get the best prices for their clients. The collective power of institutions can also act to discipline management more effectively than can small shareholders. This mitigates potential agency problems, i.e., the possibility that managers pursue their own interests, which may conflict with enhancing the wealth of shareholders.

A number of observers have commented on the relationship between institutions and corporations. Waitzer (1991, p. 9) discusses some of the contributions of institutional ownership to corporate governance, especially the institutions' success in changing the takeover process, but notes that there are still "substantial legal, political and organizational barriers [that] stand in the way of fundamental change." Por (1993) examines the role of institutions in corporate governance and recommends cooperation rather than conflict as a way of exercising fiduciary responsibility. Jarislowsky et al. (1991) offer several recommendations for better institutional-governance relations, including greater board independence, more shareholder rights activism, more effective use of

---

29 For a discussion of the potential adverse effects of private placements and bought deals on the retail market (the individual investor segment), see Andrews (1991).

share votes, and improving performance measurement. Thain and Leighton (1991) note the prevalence of companies with control block shareholders in Canada (they claim that only 15 of the top 100 companies are widely held), which enhances the importance of independent board members, who represent minority shareholders. In this environment, institutions have more ability to exert pressure on managerial discipline than do individual shareholders.

Porter (1992) estimates that institutions own 60 percent of the equity of publicly traded American companies; for the New York Stock Exchange, the figure may be as high as 70 percent (Andrews 1991). In Canada, it is estimated that institutions own 65 to 70 percent of publicly traded stocks.[30] This is a dramatic change from the 1960s, when individual investors dominated the market. Nearly a quarter of Canadians own common stocks, but much of the recent growth has been in equity mutual funds and other institutional vehicles.[31]

In terms of trading activity, institutions in Canada currently account for over 60 percent of trading volume, with even higher totals on the TSE[32] (which has the highest concentration of larger companies). Prior to the market meltdown of October 1987, which sent many individual investors scurrying for shelter, trading was split evenly between institutional and individual investors.[33] These individual investors also have an important role to play: John Bart (president of the Canadian Shareowners Association) and Pearce Bunting (president of the TSE)

---

30 See, for example, the *Globe and Mail*, November 17, 1992, p. C1. The Toronto Stock Exchange would not provide more accurate information on the grounds of confidentiality. (Telephone conversation with the TSE, July 1993).

31 See the results of the latest (at time of writing) TSE survey of individual investors entitled "Canadian Shareowners: Their Profile and Attitudes," dated December 1989.

32 *Toronto Stock Exchange Review*, April 1994, p. 2.

33 The *Financial Post*, January 4, 1991, p. 38.

agree that individual investors stabilize share prices and provide needed liquidity for smaller companies.[34]

Are stock markets myopic?

The question as to whether the growth in institutional ownership has led to a "market failure" of the type envisaged by Porter has been addressed in a number of empirical studies. For example, Bernstein (1992a) disputes Porter's thesis and presents empirical evidence that shareholders have not exhibited impatience or myopia. He cites findings (e.g., Woolridge, 1988) demonstrating that American investors value research and development expenditures and growth in capital budgets. These are examples of longer-term investments with little immediate short-term payoff, as opposed to short-term decisions, and are the kind of investments which Porter would claim will not be made by myopic markets. Woolridge found that a stock's price jumps around the time that the company announces major R&D and investment projects.

Ben-Zion (1984) measured the effect of R&D expenditures on stock prices directly, and determined that markets did react positively to such investments, but their value was not fully reflected in stock prices. That is, a stock's price did not go up as much as it should when an investment in R&D was made. A partial explanation could be that the cost of capital is higher for R&D investments than for more tangible investments, which would make the R&D investments less attractive.

The authors (Johnson and Pazderka, 1993) found that Canadian stock markets value investment in knowledge, but not fully. The market appears to reward about one-quarter to one-third of the value of R&D investment in the form of higher stock prices (a comparable magnitude to that which Ben-Zion calculated for the U.S.) See details of the study in appendix 2a.

One can conclude that markets appreciate a large part of the investment that firms make in long-term projects such as R&D. This means that markets are not myopic. Moreover, Canadian companies—in this

---

34 The *Globe and Mail*, November 17, 1992, p. C1.

respect—compete on a level playing field with their American competitors, who face similar market responses. While Canadian firms do not appear to be disadvantaged in the North American context,[35] the degree of market support they receive may be inadequate when competing against companies whose stocks trade in other countries such as Japan and Germany. We review the related evidence from other countries in chapter 4.

Differential voting shares

Different classes of common shares are issued with different voting rights, which on the surface may seem to disadvantage some shareholders. Historically, family-owned enterprises have been able to issue new equity while retaining control by means of differential voting shares (also called restricted voting shares). Such shares also served to circumvent foreign ownership restrictions, especially during the 1980s. Companies wishing to access foreign capital, but subject to foreign ownership restrictions, were able to issue new capital offshore, in the form of restricted voting shares, without violating foreign control limits.

The existence of differential voting shares is a common feature of Canadian stock markets, whereas they have historically been banned in the U.S. where shareholder democracy has more tradition. A recent count from the financial press showed that the TSE had 175 listings of such shares out of approximately 1500 listings (12 percent), the ME had 96 out of 600 (16 percent), while the VSE and ASE had no identifiable differential share issues.[36] An example of a company with multiple share classes is Unigesco, whose Class A shares have 10 votes each and Class B shares have one vote each.

---

35 For a discussion of this and other comparative international governance issues, see Johnson and Neave (1994).

36 Neither the Vancouver nor Alberta exchanges prohibit multiple share classes in principle, although there are restrictions on junior companies. Companies with multiple share classes tend to be inter-listed on the Toronto and/or Montreal exchanges, hence they do not appear in the media stock market summaries for the Vancouver and Alberta exchanges.

Several institutional investors led by William Allen and Stephen Jarislowsky repeatedly expressed concern that non- or lesser-voting shareholders might be abused by the control group (those holding the higher-voting shares), especially during takeovers. From March 1982 to October 1984, the Ontario Securities Commission prohibited the listing of restricted voting shares unless there was adequate takeover protection (Jog and Riding 1986, 65). In response, a number of companies instituted so-called "coattail provisions." A typical coattail provision ensures that all classes of common shares will receive equal treatment in the case of the transfer of ownership of some specified amount (such as a majority) of the higher-voting class. This is an example of how the market corrects its own deficiencies.

Institutional activism is taking many forms. An example of institutional reaction to the concern about shareholder rights is the statement of proxy voting guidelines drawn up by the Ontario Municipal Employees Retirement Board, which contains four basic principles:

1. All shares should have equal voting rights. We believe it is inappropriate for a fiduciary to purchase an asset if ownership rights have been subordinated.
2. All shareholders should be treated equally, which prevents "greenmail" and exclusionary tender offers.
3. Shareholders should be permitted to vote on issues that have a material financial impact upon their investments.
4. In cases where voting policies based on moral and social attitudes come in conflict with the financial integrity of the fund, the economic impact will prevail.[37]

The 1986 controversy surrounding the treatment of restricted voting shares of the Canadian Tire Corporation illustrates some of the issues at stake. The controlling Billes family owned 60 percent of the voting shares of Canadian Tire, which in total represented only 4 percent of the total shares outstanding (the remaining shares were non-voting). The Billes family attempted to tender 49 percent of their

---

37 As enunciated by James Maunder of OMERS in Jarislowsky et al. (1991).

voting shares to a group of Canadian Tire dealers, in order to transfer control of the corporation from the family to the dealer network. The family argued that this amount of shares did not constitute a majority, and hence would not trigger the coattail provision. If the takeover protection were operative, the cost of the control of the company would be about 25 times higher, since shareholders other than the Billes family would also have to be offered a premium price for their shares, and the deal would be in jeopardy. A group of non-voting shareholders, led by Allen and Jarislowsky, fought the proposal, arguing that the 49 percent represented a control position (although not technically a majority), and thus violated the spirit of the coattail provision.

The Ontario Securities Commission ruled against the Billeses. The following excerpt from OSC Chairman Stanley Beck's lengthy Reason for Decision eloquently expresses the potentially dire consequences of tampering with shareholder rights:

> A transaction such as is proposed here is bound to have an effect on public confidence in the integrity of our capital markets and on the public confidence in those who are the controllers of our major corporations. If abusive transactions such as the one in issue here, and this is as grossly abusive a transaction as the Commission has had before it in recent years, are allowed to proceed, confidence in our capital markets will inevitably suffer and individuals will be less willing to place funds in the equity markets.[38]

Clearly investor confidence is at stake in this issue, a topic that is examined further in chapter 4.

The stock market reaction to differential voting shares is manifest in relative stock prices. That is, the market includes in its valuation the relative value of the vote. For example, Robinson and White (1991) note that before the sale by the Billes family was announced, the voting shares of Canadian Tire were trading at $36 and non-voting shares at $15. Subsequently, the non-voting shares fell to $13.75, and the voting

---

38 Quoted in Brown (1989), who presents a detailed summary of the Canadian Tire case.

shares reached the high of $91. In general, the price differential between the two classes of shares is a function of the degree of takeover protection, the concentration of ownership, and the degree of voting leverage (the ratio of voting to non-voting shares). White, Robinson, and Chandra (1985) also show that the value of voting rights depends on ownership structure and the right to participate in takeovers. More formally, Maynes, Robinson, and White (1990) cite evidence showing that the share vote is worth between one to sixteen percent of total equity value.

A number of Canadian studies have analyzed the returns on differential voting shares. For example, Jog, Riding, and Seguin (1985) concluded that there were negative abnormal returns associated with issuances of restricted voting shares. This is the case because shareholders suffer a capital loss as the share prices drop due largely to a lack of takeover protection. Jog and Riding (1986) observed that a significant number of firms experienced declining share prices when restricted shares were issued. The decline was concentrated in the restricted voting shares: superior voting shares enjoyed an average positive premium of seven percent over restricted voting shares. However, Maynes (1991) found that the Ontario Securities Commission threat to delist restricted voting shares in 1981 led to negative abnormal returns on this type of shares. This suggests that the listing of these shares had value in spite of their junior ranking.

In fact, not all shareholders are concerned with the vote attached to a share. They may be more interested in sharing the company's wealth by buying the cheaper, lesser-voting shares than by paying for a vote they don't want. Such shares are simply another financial instrument with a specific purpose, which investors are free to buy or not with their eyes open. The concern that differential voting shares are necessarily bad is just another of the myths surrounding the stock market.

Summary

The tensions inherent in corporate governance arise among people, owners on the one hand and managers on the other, and controlling owners versus minority owners. The stock market acts as a dispassionate referee in this conflict, providing a vehicle (the market place for shares) through which parties can express their opinions about the way in which a corporation should be run.

This chapter explored two aspects of the stock market's role in corporate governance. First, we commented on the separation of ownership and control, and how it affects investor behaviour. In particular, we examined the myopic shareholder argument, and found that investors in Canada, and in the U.S. as well, do value long-term investments such as those in research and development, but not fully. This is important because it debunks the myth that myopic stock markets hinder economic growth. Second, we reviewed the uses and abuses of differential voting shares and their potential impact on investor confidence. We reported that such shares are valued differently from full-voting shares, and discussed the causes of price discrepancies among shares with different voting powers. This is important because it debunks the myth that such shares are necessarily bad. We now turn to one of the most contentious aspects of the stock market's role in corporate governance—the market for corporate control.

Appendix 2a: Details of Tests for Market Myopia

THE APPROACH TAKEN BY BOTH BEN-ZION (1984) and Johnson and Pazderka (1993) can be summarized in figure 8. The technique of regression analysis is utilized to measure—in quantitative terms—the sources of the variations in stock market prices. Theory suggests that if one takes a sample of companies and observes their stock prices (Johnson and Pazderka included between 47 and 54 TSE stocks in their various regression models), each will behave differently as a function of five groups of factors. First, the value of assets already in place is a major determinant of the firm's earnings and thus of its market value. Second, any market power (or monopoly power) the firm may have derived from its superior market share, superior past innovative performance, superior advertising, et cetera, enhances the earnings from these assets. Third, the firm's earnings potential is enhanced by new tangible investments (in buildings, machinery, et cetera). The fourth determinant is new intangible investment in R&D and advertising. (Data limitations made it possible to deal only with R&D expenditures.) Finally, the market value of a firm is also affected by such factors as government policies that may influence each firm differently, by "spillovers" of knowledge from research done by governments or by other firms, and

Figure 8: A Schematic View of the Determinants of Stock Prices

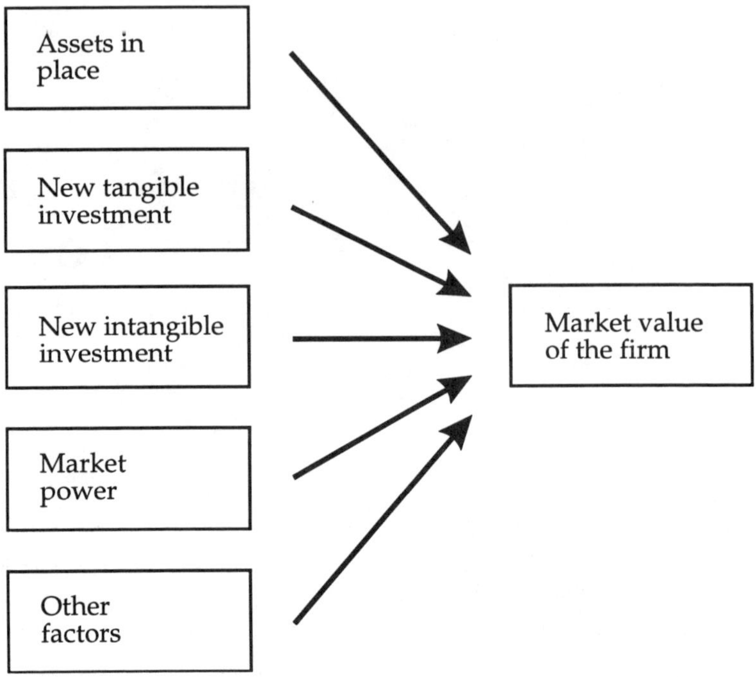

by elements of chance (luck). These, while sometimes important, cannot readily be measured and have not been included in the analysis.

Table 4 summarizes our regression results. The four explanatory variables are the book value of assets (as a proxy for assets in place), "supernormal" earnings (defined as the actual net earnings less the earnings the firm has to earn to cover its cost of capital, i.e. to provide its shareholders and bondholders with at least as good a return as they would obtain elsewhere), net investment in plant and equipment, and investment in research and development. The expected coefficient of book value is 1.0 (that is, other things equal, if the book value of assets of a firm is $1 higher than the sample average, its market value should be exactly $1 higher than the sample average). The expected magnitude of the coefficient of the market power variable is unknown, but its sign

Table 4: Regression Results, Johnson-Pazderka Study

Independent Variable	Expected Coefficients	Actual Coefficients
Book Value	1.0	1.0
Market Power	+	2
Tangible Capital Investment	6	0
Research and Development	6	2

$R^2 = 0.95$
Source: Johnson and Pazderka (1993, p. 21).

should be positive (that is the larger the firm's market share, its past innovative performance and advertising goodwill, the higher is its market value). The expected value of the coefficients on new tangible and intangible investment are about 6.0.[39]

The representative results selected from several regression models of the Johnson and Pazderka study in table 4 show that the estimated coefficient of the book value term is very close to 1.0, and that the coefficient of the earnings power term is positive, as expected. The coefficient of the new tangible investment term is positive but statistically indistinguishable from zero, while that of the new intangible investment term is 2.0. Since 2.0 is one-third of the expected magnitude, this leads us to conclude that the market does not fully value such investments.

All such studies of this type are fraught with measurement problems, so definitive conclusions are difficult. The result that the impact of new tangible investment on market value cannot be statistically distinguished from zero is problematic. Frequently, the inability of econometric studies to determine whether a particular variable "mat-

39 Roughly speaking, the coefficients of the new investment variables are an estimate of the inverse of the cost of capital. A coefficient of 6.0 implies a cost of capital of about 0.1667.

ters" is caused by the fact that the variable moves together with another variable in the same equation and one cannot therefore separate the impact of one from the other. Ben-Zion's (1984) results also showed an insignificant coefficient for new tangible investment. Our confidence in the regression results is bolstered by the indication that the model explains about 95 percent of the variations in the market value of the firms in our sample (our R^2 value of 0.95 is similar to that of Ben-Zion).

Chapter 3: Mergers and Takeovers

Introduction

MERGERS AND TAKEOVERS are two of the most contentious aspects of the functioning of the stock market. They have a key role in corporate governance in that they change corporate ownership and control. Many of them take place in an atmosphere of high drama, since entrenched managers often resist the dangers (to them) of a new ownership structure. By convention, such events are described as "hostile takeovers," but one could easily take the viewpoint of the invading company and call them "hostile defences protecting the incumbent managers who fear being replaced."

Takeovers are initiated by entrepreneurs who seek out firms whose assets are undervalued by the market because the incumbent managers do not utilize them in the most efficient manner. These entrepreneurs, or "corporate raiders," bring to the task a special insight and information which helps them identify new and more profitable opportunities for the target company.

After the takeover, the new owners typically replace the existing managers and revamp the corporate strategy; it may require closing, relocating, or selling off some plants, laying off staff, restructuring managerial responsibilities, and increasing corporate debt. The incumbent managers, of course, resist takeover attempts, even though such resistance might not be in the best interests of shareholders. We discuss the "poison pill" and a range of other devices employed for this purpose.

The measurement of benefits from takeovers is complex. Our interpretation of the U.S. and Canadian literature reviewed in this chapter leads us to conclude that they result in significant net benefits to shareholders and other stakeholders as well. This result is contrary to the popular press view that takeovers are merely the product of power struggles between greedy capitalists.

We pay close attention to the impact of takeovers on minority shareholders and, based on a survey of empirical evidence, express skepticism about the need for regulatory intervention on their behalf. Finally, we discuss the application of a new market instrument—the junk bond—in financing of takeovers. We review its treatment in the popular press as a prime example of one of the tools of the "decade of greed." We paint junk bonds in a more favourable light and highlight their contribution to bringing together people who wish to make mutually beneficial exchanges of securities with high risk and high return.

Hostile takeovers

In theory, the statutory authority of the corporate board of directors, coupled with the ability of shareholders to sell their shares if they find the corporation's performance unsatisfactory, will force managers to act so as to maximize the value of the firm, i.e., the net present value of future profits. When these mechanisms fail, a hostile takeover will take place and will remove managers who ignore shareholder interests.[40] As Bernstein (1992b, 299) notes, "the stock market is a huge voting booth in which the ballots are counted every minute of the business day."

In a hostile takeover, a "raider" bids for shares of the target firm, i.e., deals directly with the firm's shareholders, rather than with management. When the bidder gains the required votes, it assumes control of the target firm and removes the existing management. In the process,

40 In practice, many takeovers are not designed to discipline managers. Somewhat ironically, they sometimes enable managers to expand the scope of their control by directing the firm's cash flow into new ventures (Shleifer and Vishny 1988, p. 7).

the bidder often increases corporate debt, reduces employment, and sells off parts of the firm. The anticipated increase in profits of the target firm raises its value, and existing shareholders are typically paid a premium of 30 to 50 percent for their shares. Since the bidder deals directly with shareholders, it is able to remove the incumbent managers against their will. However, managers are often offered large separation payments ("golden parachutes") to reduce their opposition against the bid (Shleifer and Vishny, 1988, p. 11).

Hostile takeovers seem to be more frequent in industries subject to decline or rapid change, where managers fail to make the necessary adjustments. For example, in a sample of U.S. Fortune 500 firms, those firms that became takeover targets had a lower ratio of the market value of their debt and equity to replacement cost of physical capital (Tobin's "q") than had other firms in the sample (Shleifer and Vishny, 1988, p. 11). This suggests that corporate raiders seek out firms whose physical, human, and financial assets are not utilized in the best possible manner. By selling off some assets, reducing employment, increasing corporate debt, and replacing incumbent managers, corporate raiders may be able to increase the corporate wealth and the wealth of society as a whole. A part of the increase is transferred from employees, suppliers, and managers to shareholders even where the incumbents were reluctant or unable to do so.

The raider has to bear the transactions costs associated with the bidding process, such as the cost of acquiring information and preparing the bid. In addition, some of the raider's gains from acquisition may have to be shared with the existing shareholders of the target firm. For example, when a hostile takeover bid is initiated, small shareholders of the target firm have an option not to tender their shares and, instead, benefit from the increased profitability resulting from the policies of the new management. Alternatively, they can tender their shares at a price that reflects the anticipated higher profitability, thus depriving the raider of some of the takeover profits. To counteract this strategy, the raider may secretly accumulate some shares on the open market at a price consistent with the valuation of firm reflecting the policies of the old management.[41]

Managers of the target firm employ a variety of devices to protect themselves against hostile takeover bids. The strongest type of defense is the "poison pill." It takes a number of forms, but the common element is imposition of some costs on the bidding firm, for example by forcing it to dilute its equity holdings (by issuing new shares to shareholders other than the raider), revoking or diluting its voting rights (through a pre-determined change in voting powers triggered by the raider's arrival), or forcing it to assume unwanted financial obligations. The poison pill is usually triggered when a tender offer is made, or when a single holder accumulates some specified percentage of shares of the target firm. Managers may also attempt to prevent hostile takeovers by implementing the same measures that would be expected after the takeover, such as taking on more debt or selling off some divisions of the firm. Some of these actions increase the value of the firm, so even the threat of a takeover is potentially good for shareholders. In some cases, managers have been known to modify corporate charters to make a change in control of the firm more difficult, or to lobby for a change in legislation in favour of incumbent management.

Inco is a prime Canadian example of the use of poison pill defence. In late 1988, concerned with a potential takeover, a special shareholders' meeting approved a Recapitalization Plan, consisting of a special cash dividend of $10 per common share and a Shareholder Rights Plan. The cash dividend payment, totalling $1.06 billion, made the company less attractive, while the Shareholder Rights Plan increased the number of shares outstanding in the event that any party acquired 20 percent or more of the voting shares, thus making it more difficult for the raider to succeed. Some shareholders, especially institutional and small invest-

41 The current U.S. regulations allow the accumulation of only five to 10 percent of shares before the bidder has to make a statement declaring the intention to take over the target firm. For shares traded in Ontario (and much of the rest of Canada), the bidder becomes an insider once ten percent of the shares has been purchased, and must report all subsequent trades (although with a time lag).

ors, unsuccessfully fought this plan through the shareholders' meeting and through the courts, since it protected current management at the expense of minority shareholders who would expect to benefit from a bidding war.[42]

Reasons for takeovers and acquisitions

Acquisitions are probably the most important mechanism through which firms enter new lines of business (Shleifer and Vishny 1988, 13). In deciding which lines of business to enter, managers consider what they have to add to the firm they buy. Their contributions may include technological synergy (the whole is more than the sum of the parts), access to new markets or to capital, and their own managerial talents.

In many of the recent acquisitions of the fledgling biotechnology companies by large multinational drug companies, for example, several of these motives are combined. The biotechnology companies gain access to established marketing networks of the drug companies and to much needed cash flows to finance their R&D. The drug companies, in turn, hope to replenish their stock of innovative ideas and benefit from synergies between the traditional chemistry-based technologies and the emerging processes of biotechnology.

Most takeovers are beneficial, but not all. Managers who plan takeovers may also have their own objectives, for example, a desire to enlarge the size of their firms, to make themselves less replaceable, or to move into faster growing lines of business. The pursuit of some of these objectives does not increase the value of the firm, and, in other words, is not in the interest of the shareholders.

In this sense, Shleifer and Vishny (1988, pp. 14-15) argue that bidders overpay for companies they take over by paying for benefits which are valuable only to managers, but not to shareholders. Shareholders of the target companies benefit and shareholders of the acquiring companies lose by paying for benefits going to the acquiring company's managers. Acquisitions at inflated prices may thus be the

---

42 The *Globe and Mail,* December 10, 1988, p. B1.

most significant deviation from value-maximizing behaviour on the part of managers, at least in the view of Shleifer and Vishny.

Takeovers are initiated because of many factors, among them deregulation of many previously regulated industries, perceived synergies between the activities of the bidder and the target firm, potential economies of scale and scope to be gained from the combined operation, tax advantages from combining a tax loss of one company with a surplus of another, available managerial competence to handle unrelated lines of business, and increasing globalization of markets, which forces businesses to seek a toehold in other countries through takeovers. These are changes that enhance efficiency and add value to the economy.

In recently deregulated industries, different managerial skills and strategies are required than was the case in a tightly regulated and protected environment. Takeovers are a method of putting new management in place. The airline and telecommunications industries come readily to mind as illustrations. Innovations in takeover financing (such as the junk bond), as well as a change in behaviour of the courts and regulatory agencies in the U.S. away from protecting takeover targets have also contributed to increased takeover activity in the 1980s (Jensen, 1988, p. 28; Jarrell et al., 1988, p. 50).

Jensen (1988, pp. 28-29) draws attention to yet another factor—conflict between managers and shareholders over the payout to shareholders of "free cash flow." This is defined as cash flow in excess of that required to fund all projects that are expected to make a profit. If the firm maximizes value for shareholders, such free cash flow should be paid out. However, payment of cash to shareholders reduces the amount of resources controlled by managers, diminishes their power, and potentially subjects them to monitoring by capital markets when the firm needs new capital.

Availability of free cash flow also enables managers to expand the firm beyond the size that maximizes shareholder wealth. Growth, in turn, is associated with increased managerial compensation and opportunities for promotion. Managers can accomplish the growth objective by engaging in acquisitions, rather than by paying out the free cash flow to shareholders. In the process, they are likely to undertake low-benefit or even value-destroying mergers. In some cases, however, the spending of free cash flow on acquisitions is more beneficial than using the funds to finance low-return projects within the firm. This is one of the reasons why the bidding firms may be able to overpay for acquisitions and thus transfer some of the benefits to shareholders of the target firm.

The free cash flow theory of takeovers predicts that the acquiring firms are likely to perform exceptionally well prior to acquisition and, as a result, have free cash flow. The target firms are either those with poor management and poor performance prior to takeover, or those with large free cash flow that they have refused to pay out to shareholders.

Whether it is more beneficial to shareholders in the long run to use the free cash flow for takeovers rather than for dividend payout obviously depends on whether the takeover is a "success." The net benefits and costs of takeovers in general are also empirical questions. We now turn to the difficult question of identifying and measuring these benefits and costs.

The benefits and costs of takeovers

Scope of the debate

The debate between Robinson and Block (1991) illustrates the range of issues raised in the discussion of takeovers. Robinson argues that corporate takeovers are an example of the pursuit of opportunistic objectives, in contrast to the longer-run industrial strategies of economies such as Japan, Germany, and Korea.[43] He enumerates several social costs of takeovers, including lost jobs, deadweight costs, increased chance of bankruptcy as the bidding company increases its debt, and negative externalities affecting third parties (such as the consequence of a closure of the main industry in a town). Block replies that takeovers lead to more efficiently run companies and that some bankruptcies are inevitable and probably socially good (he gives the example of the whip and bridle maker). Takeovers are a natural extension of the forces of competition, and help to discipline management.

---

43 Johnson and Neave (1994) explain this behaviour in terms of differential corporate governance models.

The key question for the ordinary person is whether takeovers improve the efficiency and competitiveness of the economy. People also want to know how takeovers slice the corporate pie between the various "stakeholders" (shareholders of the target firm and shareholders of the bidder firm, managers, employees, et cetera). And, of course, policy questions immediately follow: Should takeover activity be restrained or encouraged? Should the internal mechanisms for safeguarding shareholder interests be strengthened instead (e.g., the boards of directors)? What type of disclosure requirements should the stock exchanges impose on those who buy shares of target companies with a view to eventually taking them over? What, if any, restrictions should be imposed on the method of financing of takeovers (e.g., are "leveraged buyouts" merely a product of unbridled greed, or a major innovation in financial markets)?

All of these issues have been extensively debated in the academic literature and in the business and popular press (where takeovers are usually deemed to be bad). The academic studies of mergers and takeovers fall into two different methodological groups (Tarasofsky and Corvari, 1991, pp. xi-xiii). In the first group are studies in the tradition of financial economics, which work with models of share price determination, typically assuming that share prices fully reflect all relevant publicly available information. In the second are studies in the tradition of industrial organization, which work with accounting data and compare the pre- and post-acquisition performance of firms involved in a takeover. Studies from both traditions conclude that takeovers on balance are good for the economy.

Empirical evidence

From the vantage point of the finance literature tradition, Jensen (1988, pp. 22-23) summarizes the principal research findings on the effects of takeovers as follows.

First, takeovers benefit shareholders of target companies. For the U.S., Jensen (1988, p. 22) estimates that, on average, they obtained premiums exceeding 30 percent, and more recently reached about 50 percent. Jarrell et al. (1988, p. 51) report that the premiums averaged 19 percent in the 1960s, 35 percent in the 1970s, and 30 percent during the period 1980 to 1985.

Second, the shareholders of acquiring companies gained on average about four percent in hostile takeovers and zero in mergers. Jarrell et al. (1988, 53) report the results of a study of 663 successful U.S. tender offers between 1962 and 1985, which estimated the gains at about one to two percent in the immediate period around the public announcement. However, the gains have declined over time and from the 1980s turned into losses for shareholders of the bidding firms. Whether this reflects managerial self-service or just bad decision-making remains to be seen.

Third, gains in economic efficiency resulting from takeovers (that is, an increase in total wealth as distinct from redistribution of resources) increased the total value of the acquired and acquiring companies on average by about eight percent.

Other findings include:

- the conclusion that management actions to prevent takeovers are generally harmful to shareholders
- golden parachutes for top managers do not usually harm shareholders
- the activities of corporate raiders generally benefit shareholders
- in the U.S. at least, mergers and acquisitions have not increased industrial concentration, and
- the gains from takeovers do not come from the creation of monopoly power.

The post-takeover restructuring of the target company typically includes a shift in corporate strategy (e.g. to meet competition or new market conditions), increased use of debt, plant closings, layoffs of managers, staff, and production workers, and reduced compensation. This is in contrast to the pre-takeover situation where managers often find it difficult to abandon major projects, relocate facilities, restructure managerial responsibilities, and close or sell off some facilities. The new top-level managers may find these actions easier because they have a fresh view of the business and no ties with current employees or the community (Jensen, 1988, p. 23). Statistics show that takeover activity is concentrated in slow-growth industries. It has been argued that takeovers are a cheaper and more efficient form of industrial adjustment ("exit" of firms from particular lines of business) than are bankruptcies.

The improvements in efficiency that come with takeovers can be threatened or delayed if the takeover is resisted by the incumbent managers. The various compensation packages ("golden parachutes") that coax managers into letting go without destructively digging in their heels are therefore useful to all concerned. There is evidence, for example, that the announcement of the adoption of severance compensation contracts by a typical firm has the effect of raising its stock price on average by three percent.[44] Stock prices go up because investors then expect to see a smooth transition to new management. However, it is in shareholder interest to extend such contracts only to those members of the top management team who play an important role in negotiating and implementing the transfer of control.

Jensen (1988, p. 21) estimates that the merger and acquisition activity in the U.S. during the decade 1977-1986 generated gains to the selling (target) firm shareholders of $346 billion (in 1986 dollars), and an additional $50 billion to the buying (bidding) firm's shareholders. This amounts to about 51 percent of all cash dividends paid to investors in the whole U.S. corporate sector during the same decade.

Takeovers and myopia

Critics argue that the fear of takeover induces managers to take decisions that overvalue current cash flow and undervalue future cash flow (myopic behaviour). The argument is that this is likely to occur when managers have only limited stock holdings in their companies or when they do not understand the determinants of share values, and when their compensation systems encourage them to increase accounting earnings rather than the value of the firm.

---

44 Jensen (1988, p. 39) notes, however, that only a portion of this increase is due to the reduction in conflict between managers and shareholders. The other portion may be a market response to the contract as a signal that a takeover bid is likely.

While admitting that such instances of myopic managerial behaviour occur, Jensen (1988, pp. 26-27) offers a number of arguments that markets (as opposed to managers) generally do not behave myopically.

First, price-earnings ratios differ among securities. For example, growth stocks and new issues of stocks of startup companies with no earnings derive their value from characteristics other than current earnings. It may be a prospect of discovery of a mineral, as in the case of startup mining companies, or the prospect of discovery of a breakthrough drug, as in the case of the emerging biotechnology companies, most of which spend, on average, around 50 percent of their sales revenues on R&D, but have yet to show a profit. In examples such as these, investors are clearly taking a longer-term perspective.

Second, there is evidence (discussed in the previous chapter) that stock prices respond positively to company announcements of increased expenditures on investment in tangible assets and negatively to announcements of reduced investment expenditures. These announcements signal at best only a potential for earnings in the future, but the stock price reaction indicates that investors have patience and are willing to wait for results.

Third, the "efficient market hypothesis," supported by a large amount of empirical evidence (reviewed in the next chapter), states that current stock prices reflect all currently available public information, not just data on current earnings. If markets were myopic, stock prices would reflect only short-term results, which is not borne out by the evidence.

Fourth, the alleged market myopia has been attributed to increases in the amount of institutional holdings, since institutional investors allegedly put pressure on management to generate high current earnings every quarter. One particular claim is that R&D spending is reduced as a result of the desire to increase current earnings. Some observers have also argued that the frequency of takeovers increases, since institutions are not "loyal shareholders." However, the U.S. evidence, cited by Jensen (1988, p. 27), indicates that increased institutional stock holdings are not associated with increased frequency of takeovers, nor with reduced R&D expenditures. Moreover, firms with high R&D expenditures do not seem more vulnerable to takeovers (which they would be if the market thought that such expenditures were wasteful), and stock prices respond positively to announcements of increased R&D expenditures, again suggesting that investors are sensitive to the long view.

One such study (Bronwyn Hall, 1990) analyzed some 600 acquisitions of U.S. firms and concluded that the acquired firms did not have higher R&D expenditures (in relation to sales) than did firms that were not acquired. There was no evidence that the post-takeover R&D spending was substantially different from pre-takeover performance. Finally, over a long period of time, the total spending on R&D by U.S. industry has been increasing simultaneously with the growth in takeover activity in the economy.

The Canadian evidence could be perhaps better characterized as the absence of any perceptible relationship at all. In table 5, we present data on Canadian Gross Expenditures on R&D (GERD), and Business Expenditures on R&D (BERD), in millions of dollars, for the period 1963-1992. GERD represents the combined R&D spending of business enterprises, federal and provincial governments, universities, and non-profit organizations. BERD is the R&D spending of the business enterprise sector alone. The last three columns in table 5 report the number of mergers and acquisitions taking place in Canada during the same period of time.

To illustrate the nature of the relationship (if any) between the trends in R&D spending and merger activity, we converted the annual BERD expenditures, measured in constant 1986 dollars, into percentage terms, with 1963=100 percent. In figure 9, we plot the results of this calculation together with the growth in the number of mergers, in percentage terms, over the same period. It seems clear that business sector R&D spending has grown fairly steadily over this period, while the number of mergers and acquisitions has fluctuated widely. This suggests that myopia-induced takeovers have not been a problem in Canada.

A simple plot of this nature of course neither proves nor disproves a causal relationship; a more conclusive analysis would require the application of multiple regression technique, and more data than are available. Nevertheless, there is as yet no case for mergers and takeovers being a major contributor to myopic underspending on R&D.

Table 5: R&D Spending and Merger Activity in Canada, 1963-1992

Year	GERD mill. $	BERD mill. $	BERD mill. 1986 $	Mergers foreign	Mergers domestic	Mergers total
1963	458	176	706	41	88	129
1964	555	229	893	80	124	204
1965	663	286	1,077	78	157	235
1966	750	313	1,125	80	123	203
1967	853	333	1,147	85	143	228
1968	905	339	1,129	163	239	402
1969	976	369	1,176	168	336	504
1970	1,071	420	1,280	162	265	427
1971	1,287	430	1,269	143	245	388
1972	1,357	462	1,291	127	302	429
1973	1,450	503	1,292	100	252	352
1974	1,666	613	1,374	78	218	296
1975	1,876	700	1,428	109	155	264
1976	2,043	755	1,419	124	189	313
1977	2,290	857	1,513	192	203	395
1978	2,576	1,006	1,679	271	178	449
1979	3,009	1,266	1,920	307	204	511
1980	3,529	1,571	2,152	234	180	414
1981	4,358	2,124	2,625	200	291	491
1982	5,128	2,489	2,830	371	205	576
1983	5,426	2,585	2,800	395	233	628
1984	6,092	2,994	3,144	410	231	641
1985	6,792	3,605	3,690	466	246	712
1986	7,347	3,996	3,996	641	297	938
1987	7,745	4,312	4,118	622	460	1,082
1988	8,254	4,618	4,214	593	460	1,053
1989	8,786	4,783	4,163	691	400	1,091
1990	9,621	5,216	4,398	676	268	944
1991	10,024	5,391	4,422	544	195	739
1992	10,289	5,512	4,478	474	153	626

Sources: Statistics Canada, Annual, *Industrial Research and Development*, Cat. 88-202; and Consumer and Corporate Affairs Canada, *Report of the Director of Investigation and Research*, Fiscal Year Ending March 31, 1993.

Figure 9: Growth of Industrial R&D Spending and Merger Activity in Canada, 1963-1991

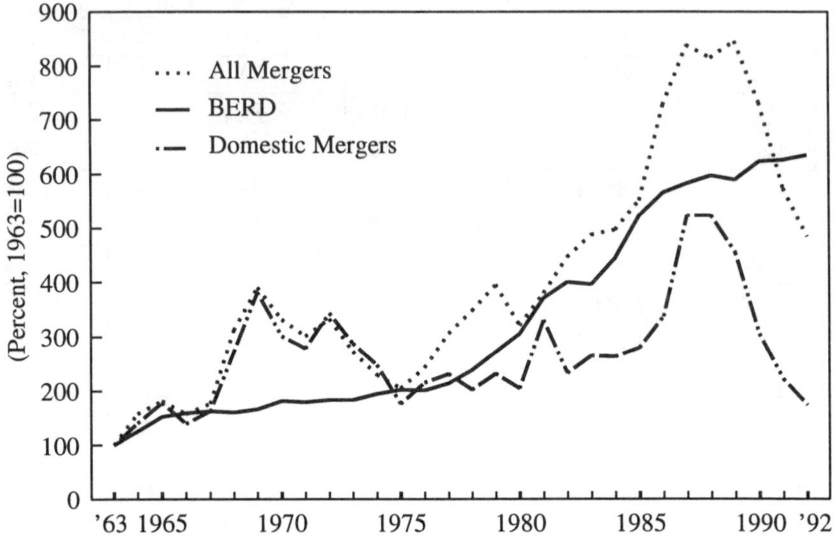

Source: Calculations based on table 5.

Wealth Transfers

Shleifer and Vishny (1988, pp. 15-16) note that corporate efficiency can improve as a result of takeovers, but draw attention to the pervasiveness of wealth transfers in the takeover process. They affect not only the shareholders of both companies, but also employees, suppliers, and managers (i.e., some shareholder gains come from reductions in wages and managerial compensation and as a result of extraction of lower prices from suppliers).

The important point is that the overall wealth in the economy increases as a result of takeovers (i.e., takeovers are not a "zero-sum game" where the gain to one party must mean a loss to another), as explained above. Shleifer and Vishny merely caution that calculations of social gains from mergers, acquisitions, and takeovers cannot rely on information on shareholder returns alone. The impact (positive and negative) on other stakeholders has to be considered as well.

The social benefits of takeovers should be calculated net of their costs, including services of the services of lawyers, investment bankers, and others organizing the transaction. Shleifer and Vishny theorize that takeovers also have consequences in the form of reduced security of long-term employment, which may lead managers to underinvest in firm-specific human capital, undertake fewer long-term projects, and be less loyal to the firm (1988, pp. 17-18). Some of these can be mitigated by explicit contractual arrangements for severance pay. The threat of immediate takeover may also generate panic, disruptions, and waste, leading to management strategies that deviate from the long-term optimum.

In the authors' view, there is a danger that considerations of this type may be used to protect the incumbent managers and ultimately to impose restrictions on takeover initiatives. Accountability of managers to shareholders should be the paramount concern and, as explained in chapter 2, the supervisory powers of the corporate boards of directors and other internal mechanisms for shareholder protection are not sufficient. Takeovers are an indispensable component of the many forms of protection stock markets offer to investors.

One step towards minimizing the costs of takeover-related disruptions would be the removal of existing constraints on share ownership by management. Shleifer and Vishny (1988, pp. 18-19) also propose that members of the boards of directors be compensated with stock, which they would be forbidden to sell until they leave the board. Finally, if hostile takeovers facilitate the adjustment of declining industries, mechanisms such as severance pay and provisions to protect labour should be strengthened. In other words, provisions for compensating the losers comprise a more efficient policy than do prohibitions on mergers and acquisitions.

Some takeovers have been motivated by tax advantages, especially the ability of one of the merging firms to reduce its taxes by absorbing the other firm's losses. Another source of tax advantage is the possibility to step-up the basis of the target firm's assets without paying corporate level capital gains. Empirical evidence suggests that tax benefits have only a minor role in explaining merger and takeover activity (Jarrell et al., 1988, p. 56).

Various authors have alleged that the premiums paid by bidders are the result of transfer of wealth from bondholders, since the bonds of an acquiring firm can drop in value if the firm pays cash for a riskier target firm. Evidence shows, however, that on average the holders of convertible bonds (bonds that can be converted by the holder into another asset, usually common stock) in the acquired firm gain from a merger. The markets presumably anticipate that the profitability of the target firm will improve after the takeover, and holders of convertible bonds will be able to participate in the increased profits as their bonds are converted into shares. Holders of nonconvertible bonds in the acquired firm and holders of convertible and nonconvertible bonds in the acquiring firm neither gain nor lose (Jarrell et al., 1988, p. 57).

The "Industrial Organization" perspective

There has been considerable discussion in the literature concerning the extent to which the gains from takeovers are due to the increased market power (domination of the market) by the new (larger) entity. In other words, does one firm try to swallow its rivals in order to become a monopoly? The emerging consensus seems to be that, except in isolated cases, increased market power cannot explain the gains from takeovers (Jarrell et al., 1988, p. 54).

For Scherer (1988, p. 70), the view that takeovers (and the market for corporate control generally) represent a remedy for the problems caused by separation of ownership and control raises some "awkward questions." For example, U.S. industry performed very well during the 1950s and 1960s, even though very few takeovers took place and the separation was firmly in place. Similarly, the economies of Japan, Germany, Switzerland, and France have performed well during the 1980s and 1990s even though hostile takeovers are practically non-existent and stock ownership is often separated from managerial control.

While Scherer's observations are plausible, their validity cannot be verified. The relevant question is whether the performance of the economies on his list would have been even better if the takeover mechanism was in place during the periods studied. It is also impossible to separate, at the level of the whole economy, the influence of takeovers (or their absence) from the many other factors, national and international, affecting the trends in indicators of aggregate economic activity.

An improvement in economic efficiency of the firm after a takeover cannot be readily inferred from the observed stock price increase alone. Studies that considered a period of one to three years after the takeover found that the acquiring firms experienced negative abnormal returns ranging from 5.5 percent to 16 percent. And, in Scherer's view, the wave of conglomerate mergers during the 1960s and 1970s represent a "widespread failure, evidenced in low returns to conglomerate firms' shareholders and extensive divestiture of ill-fitting, poorly managed subsidiaries" (1988, p. 71).

It is well known that stock prices sometimes move in a fashion approximating a random walk. It is therefore possible that a firm can become a merger target not because its managers failed to maximize profits, but because the stock market randomly (and erroneously) set its price too low. As well, any subsequent fall in prices may have more to do with such undervaluation than with the failure of the merger.

Scherer (1988, pp. 74-76) presents the results of a test of two hypotheses related to the efficiency implications of takeovers. One hypothesis suggests that if takeovers are the result of weaknesses of the incumbent management, the target firms should be less profitable than other firms in their industry group. A related hypothesis deals with the consequences of takeovers: once the inefficient management is replaced and other obstacles to efficiency are removed, the post-takeover profitability should be higher than was the pre-takeover profitability.

The test was performed with data from the U.S. Federal Trade Commission, which disaggregates company operations into detailed industry categories, thus making it possible to make well-focused comparisons between the performance of acquired units and non-acquired units of similar size in the same industry. In Scherer's analysis of the two matched groups, the takeover targets had operating income averaging 11.08 percent of assets, while the industry norm for the relevant industry groups was 12.06 percent. The takeover targets thus underperformed the industry norm by about eight percent, suggesting the presence of weaknesses in management before takeover.

Profitability was measured again over a three-year period some nine years after the takeover. The lines of business subject to acquisition through tender offer were 23 percent less profitable than were lines of business not involved in tender offers. Profitability is calculated as a ratio of operating income to assets and the value of assets of acquired companies is typically "written up" to reflect the takeover price. Much of the observed deterioration in post-takeover profitability seems to result from this accounting revaluation. Scherer (1988, p. 76) therefore concludes that "operating performance neither improved nor deteriorated significantly following takeover."

A major recent Canadian study in the industrial organization tradition (Tarasofsky and Corvari, 1991) also reported that Canadian takeovers as a phenomenon do not, on the whole, improve the performance of the affected firms. "Performance" is defined as a composite of profitability (rate of return) and risk (variability of the rate of return). Improvement occurs when the increase in the average rate of return after the takeover is greater than the increase in its variability (this is the return-risk tradeoff again), or if a decline in the rate of return is accompanied by an even greater decline in its variability. Deterioration is defined analogously. This measurement scheme reflects investors' desire for wealth and aversion to risk.

The study focused on Canadian firms that were partially acquired between 1963 and 1983, i.e., whose stock publicly traded both before and after acquisition. For a sample of over one hundred acquired firms, the average pre- and post-takeover performance was about the same. While about forty percent of the takeovers in the sample registered increased post-takeover performance, another forty percent showed a decline, and for twenty percent performance remained roughly the same. Over one-half of takeover targets with inferior pre-takeover performance registered improvement after the takeover. However, only one quarter of firms with superior pre-acquisition performance improved after the takeover (Tarasofsky and Corvari, 1991, pp. 24-25).

Opponents of takeovers sometimes argue that the bidders can offer a premium merely because the target firm is "undervalued" by the markets. The implication is that the management of the target firm should fight the takeover attempts since in the long run it can offer shareholders better returns than the opportunistic bidder. Empirical evidence is not consistent with this hypothesis; when a hostile bid is defeated, the post-defeat value of the target firm typically reverts to the (market-adjusted) level that prevailed before the bid (Jarrell at al., 1988, p. 55).

Mitchell (1991, p. 21) summarizes three studies on takeovers by the U.S. Securities and Exchange Commission. The first study finds that takeovers do discipline inefficient managers; in particular, firms making poor acquisitions are more likely to be takeover targets than firms that make acquisitions that add value. The second study concludes that increased debt burdens from leveraged takeovers force managers to more carefully scrutinize future expansion plans. According to the third study, the stock market crash of 1987 was caused in part by Congressional action to limit takeovers, suggesting that "market participants view takeovers favourably."

The treatment of minority shareholders

What happens when some shareholders of a firm are able to sell their shares at a premium during a takeover while others are left out in the cold? The concerns with fairness and investor confidence raised by Stanley Beck of the Ontario Securities Commission in the context of restricted voting shares (discussed in chapter 2) also apply to the situation of minority shareholders. This is particularly relevant in Canada, with its small number of widely held large firms (see Thain and Leighton, 1991). In the event of a takeover, control blocks may be sold by majority shareholders at a premium, bypassing minority shareholders, who do not share in the gains.

Amoaku-Adu and Smith (1991, p. 80) discuss four red flags that critics of such takeovers have raised:

1. Minority buyout transactions are "insider" bids. (Insiders are shareholders with special position and influence in the company, such as managers or shareholders with large blocks of shares). Insider bids are non-arm's-length transactions and thus there is a potential for self-dealing (doing business with close associates on non-market, favourable terms).

2. Compared to the minority shareholders, insiders may possess superior information about the value of the target company. The insider bidders may use this information asymmetry to their advantage in a takeover bid.
3. Minority shareholders are usually dispersed investors and this weakens their ability to mount any collective action.
4. Unless given special legislative voting power, the collective minority shareholder votes may not be enough to effect a change in corporate policies proposed by the controlling shareholder.

Empirical evidence assembled by Amoaku-Adu and Smith (1991) demonstrates that such concerns are groundless: minority shareholders earned more on Canadian companies taken private over the 1977-1989 period than they did in cases where the purchaser was a non-controlling shareholder. Presumably, the minority shareholders are adept at shifting their investments quickly enough to take advantage of profitable opportunities as they arise. The gains to Canadian shareholders of the target companies are not significantly different from those in the U.S., despite the closer degree of ownership and fewer multiple bids in Canada. This last factor is particularly relevant, since, according to Walkling and Edmister (1985), the existence of an opposing bid increases the size of tender offer premiums (the excess of the bid over the pre-bid market price) in U.S. takeovers.

The role of leveraged buyouts

Few aspects of the securities industry have received as much negative press as leveraged buyouts, particularly those financed by junk bonds. A leveraged buyout (LBO) is a takeover where the new owner (often current management) borrows most of the purchase price. The new owner uses the assets of the target company as collateral for the loan; that is, the buyer tells the lender that the company is worth at least so many dollars, so the lender should feel secure in financing its acquisition. Since the target company typically already has some senior debt in place, the new financing is necessarily junior.[45] When the new financing only receives a bond rating of "speculative," which is below investment grade but above default grade, the debt is usually called "junk bonds."[46]

The 1980s have become known as the "decade of greed," symbolized by the insider trading activities of Ivan Boesky and others, and fuelled by the junk bond market created by Michael Milken of Drexel Burnham Lambert. Viewed by many as the collapse of capitalism, when trading of paper replaced the trading of goods, the decade ending with the demise of Boesky, Milken et al. has been likened to a morality play. Kelley and Scott (1993) reject this interpretation. They compare the evolution of finance to technological change in other goods and services during this period, including VCRs, cordless phones, and computerized reservation systems. In their opinion, innovations in finance are just as valuable as new consumer products, and the extensive body of academic research on LBOs and junk bonds presents a picture "diametrically opposed" to the popular view of these phenomena. For example, higher shares of equity owned by management and higher debt levels improve managerial incentives and impose the "discipline of debt". Inefficient and less profitable assets and lines of business are sold off or shut down, bureaucracies are streamlined and excessive costs pared, and more efficient firms emerge.

As an added benefit, junk bonds help to restore the connection between ownership and control (discussed in chapter 2). The dismantling of conglomerates has led to more focused companies. Kelley and Scott cite evidence that LBOs have freed up large amounts of capital, and that shareholders and the economy as a whole has gained from the process. For example, one study estimated that the $1.8 trillion dollars

---

45 The seniority of debt refers to its place in the pecking order. Senior debt has a prior claim to junior debt.

46 Speculative grade bonds include three types of debt: original issue junk bonds, "fallen angels" (formerly investment grade), and "phoenixes" (formerly default grade). Common usage is to treat junk debt and speculative grade debt as synonymous, but technically this is only proper for original issue junk debt.

of U.S. corporate control transactions between 1976 and 1990 created over $650 billion of value for selling-firm shareholders (Kelley and Scott, p. 33). The incidence of LBOs financed by junk bonds was important, though not as prevalent as was popularly believed, and only three percent of such financing was used for hostile takeovers, while 22 percent was used for acquisitions in total.

Much of the bad press junk bonds have received relates to their role in aggravating the collapse of the U.S. savings & loans industry, as savings & loans managers sought out increasingly risky investments to service the high rates of interest they were forced to pay to attract investors. For many thrifts, as they are also known, real estate and junk bonds represented a disproportionate percentage of their portfolios, and the dual collapse of both real estate and junk bonds led to their demise. Nobel Prize winning economist Harry Markowitz (1992) sees the problem not in the junk bonds themselves, but rather in a system where risk and reward were separated by inappropriate regulation. The rewards accrued to the thrift managers, but the risks were borne by U.S. taxpayers through deposit insurance for which the premiums did not reflect the riskiness of the investments made by the thrifts. Hence there was little market pressure to constrain the type of investments these institutions made.

Bernstein (1992b, p. 302) concludes that the "junk bond market ... flourished because it satisfied the needs of both the investors who bought junk bonds and the relatively small companies that issued them." In the case of the issuers, who tended to be cut off from bank financing, junk bonds allowed access to new capital without diluting ownership through the selling of new stock. In the case of purchasers seeking higher yield investments, debt security (even junk debt) was preferable to an equity claim in small, unknown companies. Similarly, Markowitz (1992, p. 91) notes that:

> Clearly the junk bond market serves a useful purpose in bringing together supply and demand for such higher-risk, therefore higher-yield, securities.

Management buyout as a form of takeover deserves a separate comment. Its benefits include increased managerial incentives, savings on transactions cost due to more concentrated ownership, increased privacy, and tax savings. There is also evidence that the increase in share price during the LBO process benefits public shareholders, so that the gains from restructuring are not all captured by the acquiring management team. Potential negative consequences include the possibility of suboptimal actions to avoid hostile takeovers, potential difficulties in raising new capital, reduction of share liquidity, and the loss of managerial discipline that normally results from the pressure of public shareholders exercised through the stock market (DeAngelo and DeAngelo, 1987).[47]

LBOs have been relatively less common in Canada, probably due in part to the large number of closely held companies (see Thain and Leighton, 1991). There is no evidence to indicate that their effects have been qualitatively any different from those of the U.S. experience. The tentative conclusion here is that LBOs financed by junk bonds are not different from conventional changes in corporate control. Their inherent value must be determined using criteria discussed in chapter 2.

Summary

The last two chapters have reviewed the role of the stock market in corporate governance. This chapter has focused on the market for corporate control, and the many arguments for and against "hostile takeovers."

Viewed from the vantage point of shareholders, takeovers and acquisitions enhance the accountability of managers to shareholders and are an important mechanism through which stock market trading protects investor interests. They are a highly effective method of revitalizing the business strategy of the target companies and improving the value of their assets.

The benefits to shareholders are substantial—some U.S. estimates suggest that the value of gains from mergers and acquisitions during the decade 1977-1986 was about one-half of all cash dividends paid to

---

47 Briloff (1988) also cites examples of where LBOs can distort traditional accounting statements.

investors in the whole U.S. corporate sector during the same decade. Contrary to some assertions in the popular press, empirical evidence indicates that increased market dominance (or monopoly power) is not an important source of gains from takeovers.

While most of the shareholder benefits result from improved post-merger performance of the target companies, some of them come at the expense of the incumbent managers and other stakeholders. We have reviewed the various forms of poison pill and other takeover defences employed by managers, and the use of "golden parachutes" and similar arrangements for mediating the conflict between managers and shareholders. In our view, they are preferable to regulatory restrictions on takeovers which may deprive shareholders of potential benefits.

We have examined the evidence on the relationship between mergers and acquisitions on the one hand and corporate investment in long-term growth, exemplified by R&D spending, on the other. In our view, the argument that mergers and takeovers contribute to myopic underspending on R&D does not stand up to close scrutiny.

The last part of the chapter pays considerable attention to leveraged buyout takeovers financed by junk bonds. We view them as a financial innovation that allows access to new capital to investors cut off from bank financing because of the riskiness of their ventures. The evidence indicates that leveraged buyouts and junk bonds may not be as evil as portrayed by the media, and that leveraged buyout takeovers are not qualitatively different from conventional takeovers.

The contribution of stock market to corporate governance is one of its many social benefits. In the next chapter we turn to a more general examination of the market's performance, with emphasis on the efficiency of the Canadian stock market.

Chapter 4: The Efficiency of the Canadian Stock Market

Introduction

IN CHAPTER 1 WE STATED that the principal role of stock markets is to act as an intermediary between lenders and borrowers, and we emphasized the market's primary functions: providing a central market place, pooling funds, and spreading risk. In this chapter we explore the economic consequences of this intermediation role. It is important to ask the question, "How well does the market do its job?" and we use the concept of "efficiency" to measure this performance.

The intermediation role fundamentally relates to the market's ability to facilitate capital formation, that is, to ensure that the economy's resources are allocated in the most productive manner. The extent to which the market is successful in this endeavour is a measure of its allocative efficiency. A market's degree of allocative efficiency corresponds closely to an economy's international competitiveness, so an understanding of the Canadian stock market's performance in this regard is important.

We first define the meaning of the term "efficiency," and then examine the evidence on the efficiency of the Canadian stock market. We look separately at external efficiency (how well stock prices reflect information) and at internal efficiency (how costly it is to operate the market). We conclude that Canadian markets perform nearly as well as their larger American counterparts on both counts, and we then compare North American markets to their international competitors. We see that there are some competitive disadvantages relative to Japan and Germany, but that these appear to be based more on the behaviour of Canadian business people than on any inherent weakness of Canadian capital markets.

The concept of efficiency

Baumol (1965, p. 3) lists several properties of stock markets which "render them specially suitable to serve as capital resource allocators." They include: guidance to business management, for example by providing information on the current cost of capital; access to large numbers of (often small) capitalists; administratively simple funds transfer mechanisms; an evaluation by the market of the firm's future prospects; and the ability to finance long-term projects using funds provided, in many instances, for only limited periods of time (this is the "magic" of the secondary market).

The concept of allocative efficiency is so all-encompassing that measuring it is hard. It helps to break allocative efficiency down into two more manageable concepts: external efficiency and internal efficiency (West, 1975).

A market is externally efficient if prices of securities reflect relevant information, and if they react quickly to reflect the effects of new information about the firm's products, its costs, its management, its dividend policy, et cetera. If the value of a stock does not reflect such information, investors are backing the wrong horses, and this is bad for the economy. For example, if a struggling new computer firm clearly demonstrates that it has the best product on the market and if investors ignore this, they will underinvest in the firm and the firm may go under. Consumers could suffer because of the mistakes of investors.

In an efficient market, then, prices act as valid signals for resource allocation, both to investors investing in securities and to corporate managers engaged in capital formation. So, for example, an investor choosing among alternative stocks can have confidence that their prices fairly reflect their relative values. At the same time, the corporate manager considering alternative investments can have confidence that funds will be available for those that are profitable, since the market will recognize and value those profitable investments. As Baumol (1965, p. 67) puts it, "rewards and punishments would be meted out by the market and management's collective nose kept to the grindstone by anticipated future capital needs." External efficiency is also variously known as market efficiency, informational efficiency, and pricing efficiency.

A close relative of external efficiency is mean-variance (or Markowitz) efficiency: a portfolio is said to be "mean-variance efficient" if it provides the highest prospective return for a given level of risk (or, alternatively, the lowest level of risk for a given level of prospective return). Mean-variance efficiency is at the heart of what is known as modern portfolio theory, which includes equilibrium pricing models such as the capital asset pricing model (CAPM) and the arbitrage pricing theory (APT).[48] Basically, such models find ways to provide investors with an optimal mix of reward and risk (as we discussed in chapter 1). In more mundane usage, the concept of diversification (reducing risk by not placing all eggs in one basket) is very closely related to modern portfolio theory.

Mean-variance efficiency is relevant in the present context because risk and return are important characteristics of a security, and hence they should be reflected in its price. That is, riskier investments should provide a higher return, so their initial price should be lower. As well, "because the stock market makes diversification easy and inexpensive, the average level of risk-taking in society is enhanced" (Bernstein, 1992b, p. 300). The growth of mutual funds is a direct consequence of investors' need to diversify, and to achieve mean-variance efficiency. As we saw in chapter 1, one of the stock market's major social benefits is aiding investors in finding the right mix of reward and risk.

---

48 The CAPM is a model in which required returns for a stock are a linear function of systematic (non-diversifiable) risk. The APT is a less restrictive model in which required returns are a linear function of several variables, not necessarily derived from a rigorous theoretical model.

A market is said to be internally efficient if the costs of effecting transactions are minimized. Costs are defined here to include the resources spent on acquiring and processing information (time and money), as well as the obvious costs of trading. This concept of efficiency is also known as operating or transactional efficiency. Figures 5 and 6 in chapter 1, which show the benefits of adding a central market, are crude representations of internal efficiency.

External and internal efficiency are linked, for, intuitively, a market is more likely to be price efficient if it is well functioning on the operating level. Fama (1970, 1991) expressed this notion more formally. All markets would be externally efficient if information and transactions costs were zero and all participants held common beliefs on the implications of information. More realistically, we define markets as being efficient if market transactions take account of all available information (no matter how high the transactions costs may be). A "sufficient" number of investors must have access to information, and no investor can consistently make better evaluations of the information (1970, pp. 387-388).

Efficiency is essential for capital formation; that is, the economy will not grow as quickly if the market is not efficient. Investors will be more willing to provide their funds to the market if they have confidence that their funds will be invested productively. External efficiency is present if the prices paid for stocks truly reflect the underlying value and risk exposure. Internal efficiency is achieved when market frictions are minimal, so that the maximum volume of investors' funds reaches the best investment opportunity. This chapter explores how Canadian stock markets meet these requirements.

External efficiency: Can one "beat the market?"

Markets are said to be (informationally) efficient if prices reflect all relevant information, that is, the information affecting stock prices (Fama, 1970, 1991). If a market is efficient, one cannot predict the stock price any better than can other investors. There is no information sitting around that one could use to consistently outguess other investors, since any information about the future prospects of a company has been fully analyzed and the stock price has adjusted to reflect this information. Unless new information comes along, there is no reason to expect the stock price tomorrow to be any different than it is today.

Something known as the weak form of the efficiency hypothesis suggests that it is impossible to predict a stock's price (determine that the stock is undervalued or overvalued by the market) on the basis of its prior trading history, such as price and volume. The semi-strong form implies that such prediction is impossible even on the basis of all publicly available "fundamental" information, such as past and present earnings, revenues, management changes, et cetera. The extreme version of strong form efficiency postulates that market prices incorporate all information, whether or not it is publicly known (such as dividend changes and new investment plans). In other words, one cannot predict a stock's price at all, since the market always values all securities as correctly as the available information permits.

Fama's (1970) summary of the empirical evidence to that date indicated that U.S. markets were efficient at least in the weak and semi-strong forms, but that some insiders such as market specialists could "beat the market." In the later work (1991), Fama concluded that U.S. markets seem to exhibit some anomalous results, such as the small firm effect (small firms tend to have relatively higher returns than one would expect from their risk level) and the price-earnings effect (low P/E firms do better than expected). The importance of these anomalies cannot be determined with much confidence, since there are measurement errors, and the tests make it impossible to distinguish whether market efficiency is lacking, or the underlying pricing model does not adequately characterize the market.

The event studies (investigations where the researcher attempts to isolate the response of a stock price to a specific relevant "event," such as a stock split, takeover threat, or dividend announcement) he reviewed supported earlier evidence that new information is rapidly impounded into share prices. The tests of private information confirmed that corporate insiders do have information that is not fully reflected in price (which is why markets have restrictions on insider trading, as discussed in chapter 6). Professional investment managers (such as mutual fund and pension plan managers) who may be expected to have superior information do not appear to have the ability to capitalize on it consistently (i.e., beat the market all the time).

Fama's conclusion is that the U.S. markets appear to be reasonably efficient in the informational sense. Prices do reflect information, and the apparent anomalies detected by academic studies can be questioned on the grounds of methodological problems such as measurement errors and model specification. Bernstein (1992b, p. 304), in reviewing the U.S. evidence on market efficiency, concludes "[i]f the walk is more random than ever, information must be moving faster, prices must be holding closer to intrinsic values, and outguessing the market must be growing increasingly difficult." That is, if markets are really becoming better at absorbing information, stock prices should appear to move randomly. This randomness reflects the random pace at which new information hits investors.

Tests of efficiency of Canadian markets

Weak form efficiency

Weak form efficiency suggests that stock prices reflect the history of stock market trading. Weak form tests implicitly make a judgment on the value of technical analysis, a trading strategy in which future price movements are predicted from past price and volume data. To refute the claims of technical analysts, advocates of market efficiency have devised a variety of tests. These tests typically take the form of returns pattern tests (determination whether the future can be predicted on the basis of past pattern of returns) and filter tests (filter rules are trading strategies where buy or sell decisions are triggered by persistent up or down price moves that exceed a pre-determined "filter" or pre-specified minimum size of price change).

Canadian tests of returns patterns are consistent with the U.S. results, and contrary to the claims of technical analysts, stock price changes generally do not have a systematic time pattern, with the exception of an apparent weekend effect (prices regularly tend to rise on Fridays and drop on Mondays). Chamberlain, Cheung, and Kwan (1988) confirmed this day-of-the-week effect, especially for less heavily traded stocks. However, making use of this knowledge (as well as the knowledge of many similar anomalies discussed below) is difficult since the costs of stock-broker commissions may offset any gains made by trading. Jaffe and Westerfield (1985) also confirmed the presence of the weekend effect in Canadian stock market trading. Lawson (1980) tested a variety of filter rules for market professionals on the TSE and concluded that such trading strategies were inferior to a buy-and-hold strategy (which is the strategy of the investor who believes that information is already reflected in the stock's price). Most of these studies agree that Canadian markets appear to be efficient in the weak form sense.

Considerable effort has been directed at cross-sectional predictability of returns, in other words, at determining how shareholder gains should differ from one company to another. The technique researchers generally follow is to devise a trading strategy and see if it beats the market. The trading strategy can take any form from the most simple to the most sophisticated. One such strategy is based on a model of how the market should work, known as the capital asset pricing model (CAPM). Morin (1980) applied the CAPM to Canadian data, but did not succeed in explaining returns, mainly because of data limitations and measurement problems. Robinson (1993b) replicated the principal U.S. empirical studies with Canadian data, and found less support for the validity of the CAPM in Canada than in the U.S. Calvet and Lefoll (1980) came to a similar conclusion and hypothesized that the effects of seasonality (systematic patterns such as the January effect) and the failure to account for the effect of firm size on returns are responsible for the lack of success of the CAPM in explaining returns. This does not mean that the market is not efficient, only that the CAPM is unable to describe it accurately.

One possible reason for the weaker performance of the CAPM with Canadian data is a greater incidence of thin trading in Canada than in the U.S. (see Fowler, Rorke, and Jog, 1980). Stocks that are thinly traded (do not trade often) create statistical problems in measuring the difference between returns on the thinly traded stock and returns on the market index at a point in time. This results in a weakening of any statistical inference from such tests.

The arbitrage pricing theory (APT) model is similar to, but less restrictive than (because of its underlying assumptions), the CAPM. There are two approaches to testing the market efficiency using the APT. In the first approach, the data are sorted by statistical similarity (common "factors"), and then these factors are tested to determine whether they help explain stock returns. The second approach considers a number of macroeconomic factors (such as changes in GNP and interest rates) and examines whether and how they affect stock returns. Hughes (1984), Abeysekera and Mahajan (1987), and Smith (1993) find only weak support for the APT in Canada using the first procedure. Otuteye (1991) finds somewhat stronger empirical support for models working with the macroeconomic factors.

A number of Canadian studies have focused on the apparent anomalies that emerged from the asset pricing model tests. An anomaly is an empirical regularity that is inconsistent with the theory, or, to put it another way, the market is not behaving exactly as the theory predicts. This suggests either that the market is not efficient or that the models used are not close enough to reality to describe it. One example of an anomaly is the day-of-the-week effect. Jog (1988) conducted an exhaustive study of several such anomalies, including negative Monday returns, the month-end effect (returns are highest around the last trading days of the month), the January effect (returns are higher in January than in any other month), and the small firm effect (also called the small-cap effect: smaller firms tend to have higher returns on a risk-adjusted basis than do larger firms). He concluded that the time-related anomalies could not be profitably exploited because of transactions costs, but that there were opportunities with size-based anomalies (the emergence of small-cap mutual funds is one response to this opportunity). However, Mittoo (1991) finds that the size effect largely disappeared in Canada around 1982, as the market learned from academic research. Other studies conclude that there is a strong interaction among many of these anomalies, with the January effect apparently dominating (see, for example, Foerster and Porter, 1993). The implication of these tests is that there does not seem to be any persistent, exploitable market inefficiency in Canadian markets.

In summary, then, results of the studies of weak form efficiency, augmented by returns predictability tests, in Canada are qualitatively similar to those in the U.S. Simple technical trading rules are shown to be unprofitable, and many of the anomalies documented in U.S. studies are confirmed for Canada as well (although the ability to profitably exploit them is doubtful). The weaker empirical support for the asset pricing models in Canada is not disturbing—it merely says that, at least in theory, prices may be deviating from value. However, the many data weaknesses and measurement problems associated with these tests make any conclusions tentative at best.

Semi-strong form efficiency

Unlike the weak form tests, which only test the market's ability to react to historic information, the semi-strong form tests also include all publicly available information, such as new products, a change in dividend policy, et cetera. Semi-strong form tests typically take the form of event studies investigating how stocks respond to such "events" as stock splits, takeover threats, or dividend announcements. If markets are efficient (in the semi-strong sense), stock prices respond immediately, and the long-term impact of the event in question is fully reflected in the price change.

The evidence on such efficiency is mixed. For example, Porter (1993) studied the behaviour of returns around the time of stock splits, but his findings were ambiguous due to instability of the regression coefficients of the pricing model employed. Other Canadian event studies include Charest (1980), who found evidence of inefficiencies (incomplete market response) around the dates of dividend announcements. In contrast, the findings of Calvet and Lefoll (1985) supported semi-strong efficiency around the dates of merger announcements. Kryzanowski (1979) concluded that there are inefficiencies relating to suspensions of trading in listed stocks imposed as a result of negative news, but no inefficiencies if the suspensions were due to positive news. Recently, Hennessey (1993) uncovered inefficiencies related to earnings forecast revisions.

The evidence on semi-strong form efficiency in Canadian markets is therefore mixed. One specific problem with these tests may be that stock prices respond with delays. Methodological problems associated with tests of the efficiency hypothesis make any conclusions tentative. For example, Kryzanowski and Zhang (1993) demonstrate that the apparent abnormal returns associated with stock splits may be due to mis-measurement of time-varying volatility of stock prices, and not to market inefficiency.

One study not subject to this criticism is the analysis of insider trading by Suret and Cormier (1990). They did not use the event study methodology but employed an "Insider Confidence Index" developed by Richardson Greenshields. It provides a standardized report on the pattern of buying and selling by corporate insiders over the six months preceding the release of the information. During most of this six month period, such inside trades would be public knowledge (since Canadian regulations require that all trades by insiders be reported), so presumably the market, if efficient, would have already accounted for any information contained in the Insider Confidence Index. Suret and Cormier found, however, that stocks being bought by insiders outperformed both those sold by insiders and those bought and sold by the market as a whole. With some caveats regarding transactions costs, Canadian stock prices "take their time" (p. 89) adjusting to knowledge of insider trades.

Strong form efficiency

A number of Canadian studies have tested the strong form efficiency hypothesis (i.e., the notion that stock prices reflect private, as well as public, information). Such tests try to determine if one can beat the market using information that is not generally available to the investing public. Lawson's (1980) study of filter rules analyzed professional traders' transactions, and concluded that they were unable to beat a buy-and-hold strategy. Kryzanowski's (1979) analysis of trading suspensions (instances when a company's stock is temporarily suspended from trading by the exchange) suggests that regulators could have profited from them. Baesel and Stein (1979) found evidence that insiders could consistently outperform other investors on both the buy side and the sell side. In contrast, Calvet and Lefoll (1980) and Jog (1986) determined that mutual funds and pension plans were unable to earn superior returns, as predicted by the strong form efficiency hypothesis.

In summary, there does appear to be some evidence that private information can be used to beat the market. This should not be surprising, since it is a tall order for a market to consistently anticipate news before it is released. This result, then, is not disquieting, as very few people have access to such information, and, by and large, they are constrained from acting on it to the detriment of other investors.

Internal efficiency

The stock market consists of two components: the primary market, where new share capital is raised, and the secondary market, where these shares subsequently trade. To attract listings, stock markets must be more concerned than ever with internal efficiency, in both primary and secondary markets, or companies will take their business elsewhere. The growth of global capital markets makes it possible for some large companies such as Bell Canada to be listed on exchanges around the world, so these companies will tend toward cost efficient markets.[49] Internal efficiency refers to the costs of performing transactions. Other things equal, companies will issue shares and investors will trade them in the market offering the best price.

Internal efficiency also encompasses factors other than price. A fair, equitable and visible market enhances investor confidence. Kirzner (1990, p. 44) identifies six factors necessary for a "quick execution-fair price" trading system:

1. good liquidity,
2. enhanced price discovery process,
3. fair and equal treatment of all participants,
4. maximum trading facilitation,
5. minimum trading costs,
6. no incentives or opportunities for trading abuses.

---

49 As of the date of its 1992 Annual Report, BCE common stock was listed on the Toronto, Montreal, Vancouver, Paris, Frankfurt, Duesseldorf, Tokyo, Zurich, Basel, Geneva, Amsterdam, London, and New York stock exchanges.

It is worth emphasizing that several of the factors listed have nothing to do with dollar costs of trading on a given market. For example, Andrews (1993) claims that the competitiveness of Canadian capital markets is threatened by "antiquated backrooms" (i.e., the infrastructure that handles payments, clearings, and settlements).

The primary and secondary markets have distinct roles. While new capital is raised in the primary market, this could not occur as efficiently in the absence of well-functioning secondary markets. Secondary markets not only provide needed liquidity (stocks can easily be converted into cash), but also encourage risk-taking by investors because liquidity confers flexibility (stocks may be sold at any time). Secondary markets also provide valuable pricing information to the primary market, i.e., they help determine at what price new stock issues should be offered (Van Horne, 1984, p. 6). For example, if Bell Canada wanted to issue new stocks, it would refer to its stocks already trading to determine the issue price.

In addition, as Baumol (1965) noted, the existence of secondary markets permits financing of long-term projects by investors with short-term investment horizons (again, because the short-term investor can sell the shares at any time and other investors will buy them). The key here is that such liquidity does not tie any single investor to a particular stock forever. This distinct role of the secondary market is not understood by many critics, such as Walter Stewart (1992), who frequently cite the much larger size of the secondary market as evidence of the failure of the primary market. We examine the internal efficiency of the two markets separately in recognition of their different but complementary roles.

Primary market efficiency

The efficiency of the primary market depends on the costs associated with issuing new securities, whether for established companies or for new entrants (initial public offerings). Primary market financing costs are known as flotation costs. They can take the form of the underwriter's spread (the net profit between the proceeds of the issue from the public sale and the amount which the issuing company receives), legal and administrative costs, and underpricing (setting an issue price low enough to be able to sell the issue but below the underlying value offered by the issuing company). In the Bell Canada example just mentioned, Bell would probably agree to accept a small discount from the current market price in order to sell the new issue.

Hunter (1986) discusses the reasons why Canadian flotation costs have traditionally been higher than the U.S. costs (e.g., higher distribution costs due to thinner markets, and hence fewer potential purchasers). Recently, however, "bought deals" (first initiated by Gordon Capital) have made primary financings more competitive by breaking up the long-established arrangements between corporations and their investment bankers. In a bought deal, the underwriter assumes the price risk for the issue (that is, the risk that the issue will not sell at the issuing price), whereas with a traditional underwriting the risk remained largely with the issuing company. Hunter claims that bought deals have reduced flotation costs to about one percent of the issuing price compared to two percent or more for the traditional underwriting process. Hunter also notes that private placements (i.e., issuing securities to a small number of institutional investors) have become a cost-effective alternative for smaller companies without access to more competitive international markets. This is another example of how the stock market is continually discovering new ways to be efficient and to pass the savings on to the public.

A number of studies have analyzed the alleged underpricing of Canadian initial public offerings (IPOs) which are new stock issues by companies that do not already have stock trading on the exchange. Jog and Riding (1987) estimated an average underpricing for Canadian IPOs over the 1971-1983 period in the range of nine to 11.5 percent of the underlying value, which compares favourably with analogous U.S. values of between 11 and 18 percent. Its magnitude was greater for more thinly traded securities and for firms in the industrial sector. Krinsky and Rotenberg (1989) identified comparable evidence of IPO underpricing, the magnitude of which depends on a variety of signalling mechanisms, including fractional ownership by the entrepreneur and the selection of prestigious underwriting services. Rotenberg (1990) reviewed the reasons for IPO underpricing, and concluded that factors such as the book value of assets, the quantity and quality of information revealed, the quality of the auditor and underwriters, and the use of offering proceeds were significant determinants (in a statistical sense). According to Srivastava (1990), both the underwriter compensation and the degree of underpricing are lower for private placements than for public offerings.

Underpricing of IPOs is not necessarily bad. As mentioned above, a company may willingly accept a discount in order to sell a new issue. With initial public offerings, in which there is no outstanding stock already trading on the market (unlike the case of Bell Canada), such a discount is even more necessary.

Secondary market efficiency

The efficiency of the secondary market depends on the level of transactions costs, which include dealer commissions as well as information costs (searching and monitoring the performance of listed companies). The lack (until recently) of broadly based, publicly available analysts' forecasts and other investment advisory services has historically impaired Canadian investors. This is less of a problem currently with the development of sources such as ValueLine's Canadian Edition, InfoGlobe, Infomart, and a variety of other commercial electronic and hard copy services.

One of the most visible transactions costs is the bid-ask spread (the difference between what a dealer will pay for a stock and what he or she will sell it for). Hunter (1986) reports that Canadian secondary markets are thin and illiquid compared to those in the U.S., and consequently have higher bid-ask spreads (dealers require more profit for assuming the higher risk of thinly traded securities). Thin markets also exhibit more price pressure (i.e., a single offering tends to depress prices) as there are fewer offsetting positions to absorb (especially large) trades. Griffiths (1993) studied the level of investor trading for Canadian securities over the period 1975-1987. Systematic thin trading was related to market capitalization (smaller firms trade less often), to share price (lower-priced shares trade less often), and to calendar date (trading is less frequent on Mondays and Fridays, more frequent on Tuesdays and in January and February).

Hunter (1986) notes that the introduction of negotiated commission rates in Canada in 1983 and price pressure from interlisted shares (that is, trading of the same stock on more than one exchange) have reduced the bid-ask spread in Canada considerably, although much evidence suggests that commission costs have increased for retail investors while declining for institutional clients. The introduction of discount brokerages, where customers buy trading services, but no advice or other services, helped offset this discrepancy, and the proliferation of electronic quotation and trading systems will further reduce commission costs. This makes investing more profitable for all investors and the stock market more attractive as a place to invest money.

Schulman's (1989) comparison of bid-ask spreads for securities traded on the Toronto and New York Stock Exchanges shows that Canadian stocks typically traded with higher spreads, with the average spread of 0.67 percent in Toronto being almost twice the New York spread of 0.35 percent. Robinson and White (1991) compared block trades (trades of at least 10,000 shares) of interlisted securities (securities listed in Toronto as well as on the New York and/or American Stock Exchanges). No systematic preference for one market over the other was found. The implication of this finding is that Canadian stock markets seem to be reasonably efficient in comparison with those of the U.S.

Implications for Canadian capital formation and competitiveness

The efficiency gap between Canadian and U.S. markets has been narrowing, due in part to a variety of institutional, technological, and competitive factors. Other evidence, such as that presented by Johnson and Pazderka (1993) discussed in chapter 2, suggests that the Canadian market may not be efficient in placing full value on intangible investments such as research and development and worker training, but that U.S. markets fare no better. This is a form of "acid test" of allocative efficiency, and it would be useful to review the evidence from other countries as well, especially as Canadian trade increasingly expands beyond our traditional major trading partner to the south.

The cost of capital is the hurdle rate for investment decisions. A company or country with a lower hurdle rate will be more competitive because it can profitably proceed with investment projects that would have to be rejected by companies or countries with higher costs of capital. The role of the stock market is central here, because if the market does not place full value on corporate investments, it amounts to the same thing as raising the hurdle rate investment projects must meet in order to be accepted as profitable. That is, a company may have to issue more shares than is necessary to fund new investments if the market does not fully value, in terms of the price of the shares, the new investment.

Pecaut (1993) compared the cost of capital for Canadian companies to those in other major industrialized countries. While the Canadian cost of capital was comparable to that of the U.S., it was significantly higher than in Germany, Japan, and the industrializing countries of Asia. Figure 10 shows the respective real cost of capital (nominal cost less the domestic inflation rate) for Canadian and Japanese companies for a variety of industries. Only in "heavy manufacturing" do Canadian companies have a comparative advantage, and in most industries the cost disadvantage they face is substantial.

Pecaut alleges that there are four fundamental reasons for the cost differential: a lower savings rate in Canada, higher capital gains taxes for equity investors, higher risk associated with our resource-based economy, and differences in corporate structure, forcing Canadian companies to use more higher-cost equity financing.[50] Pecaut fails to recognize, however, that Canada has one of the most generous system research and development tax incentives in the world. Also, in spite of these potential disadvantages, Pecaut's analysis fails to tell us why Canada has one of the highest investment growth rates in the industrialized world.

McCauley and Zimmer (1989) report similar results based on comparing the nominal U.S. cost of capital for a variety of investment decisions over a period of time with the cost of capital in Japan, Germany, and the U.K. These comparisons are shown in table 6. It is evident that for most investment decisions the U.S. is severely handicapped

50 See Johnson and Neave (1994) for a fuller discussion of this factor.

Figure 10: Cost of Capital for Canadian and Japanese Companies, 1982-1988

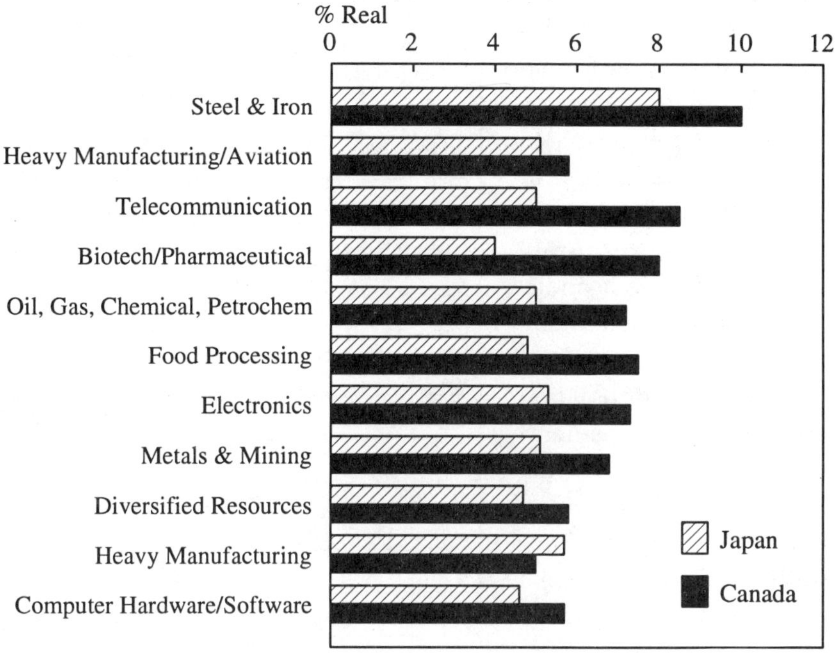

Source: Canada Consulting Group analysis using Callard Madden Associates data.

relative to its major competitors, particularly Japan and Germany. Canada's capital costs are comparable to the U.S.; hence one can infer that Canada's competitiveness is similarly potentially impaired.

McCauley and Zimmer consider four possible explanations for the higher U.S. cost of capital, including differences in tax rates and personal savings efforts, macroeconomic stability, and institutional differences in capital structure. This list is almost identical to that produced by Pecaut for Canada, but McCauley and Zimmer reject different tax structures as unimportant, and accept the other factors with varying degrees of confidence.

Capital formation and international competitiveness are also addressed by Jog and Srivastava (1993), in their survey of senior managers of Canadian companies. They identified the lack of internally generated funds as the single largest impediment to capital formation. In addition, managers reported a reluctance to access external funds. In well-functioning securities markets, corporate managers should be indifferent between internally and externally generated funds (except for flotation costs, control considerations associated with the issuance of new securities, and a reluctance to submit to the discipline of public disclosure requirements). Managers' estimates of the cost of externally generated capital were only marginally higher than those of internally generated capital, suggesting that a behavioral rather than economic motive is at play. This "wedge" between internal and external financing represents a social loss domestically (due to foregone investment opportunities) and a competitive disadvantage internationally.

Table 6: Cost of Capital for Various Projects, 1988 (Values in Percent)

Equipment and machinery with physical life of 20 years	
United States	11.2
Japan	7.2
Germany	7.0
United Kingdom	9.2
Factory with physical life of 40 years	
United States	10.2
Japan	5.0
Germany	5.4
United Kingdom	7.9
Research and development project with 10 year payoff lag	
United States	20.3
Japan	8.7
Germany	14.8
United Kingdom	37.4
Expensed item with physical life of 3 years	
United States	40.4
Japan	34.9
Germany	34.8
United Kingdom	37.4
Land	
United States	10.6
Japan	5.4
Germany	4.7
United Kingdom	7.7

Source: McCauley and Zimmer (1989).

Pecault (1993) recommends a variety of tax incentives and a restructuring of Canada's national institutional arrangements as remedies for the situation as he perceives it. Jog and Srivastava (1993) propose productivity improvements to enhance internally generated funds and to decrease reliance on external funds. The evidence on the relative efficiency of Canadian stock markets presented above, along with the demonstrated growth in investment that Canada has experienced, suggest that this apparent problem is more perceptual than substantive. In spite of a number of technical potential impediments, and a globally uncompetitive environment engendered by high borrowing to finance government deficits, Canadian stock markets are still able to promote and facilitate economic growth.

Summary

This chapter has examined the question, "How well does the stock market work?" The answer to this question requires a review of how efficient the market is in, first, setting the price of stocks, and, second, doing so at minimum operating cost.

The evidence indicates that Canadian market efficiency is comparable to that of U.S. markets, but in some respects we may be at a potential competitive disadvantage relative to the Japanese and European markets. Nevertheless, one should not be too critical of the Canadian stock markets—internationally comparable data are more readily available for financial markets than for other markets or for government activity; hence, most of the published analytical studies apply to them. This does not mean that other markets or the governments in Canada and the U.S. are necessarily any less efficient than those in Japan or Europe.

The recommended remedies for the perceived competitive disadvantage of Canada range from emulating other markets to increased government intervention. The recent slowdown in the Japanese and European economies render their models somewhat less attractive; indeed, there is even evidence that Japanese industry may be turning from its traditional norms to a more North American style of management.[51] With respect to increasing the role of government, the limitations of government intervention are addressed in chapter 7. On balance, we conclude that stock markets are not perfect but do their job adequately and do not require major tinkering.

---

51 See, for example, "Economic eclipse darkens outlook for Japan Inc.," The *Globe and Mail*, Monday, October 4, 1993, p. B1; and "The Tokyo Exchange as a Free Market?" *New York Times*, Sunday, August 29, 1993, p. F11.

Chapter 5: Emerging Markets

Introduction

THE EXCITEMENT THAT BEGAN with the collapse of Communism and the fall of the Berlin Wall is still being felt in the former centrally planned economies of eastern Europe, as they feel their ways toward market-driven economies. Central to this evolution is the development of a financial system to help these dormant economies become competitive. A financial system is necessary to perform the functions of mobilizing and distributing savings among competing uses, allocating and pricing risks, and facilitating transactions.

The Canadian system of financing, much like the systems of the U.S. and U.K., is variously described as "stock market dominated," or as "individualistic capitalism," or simply as the "Anglo-American system." By contrast, the systems of Japan, Germany, and other European countries are characterized as "bank-dominated," or as "communitarian capitalism," or simply as the "European-Japanese system."

In this chapter, we discuss the strengths and weaknesses of the two systems. As a case study, we draw upon the still evolving experience of the former centrally planned economies of eastern Europe and analyze selected "emerging markets" in the developing and newly industrialized countries.

In eastern Europe, the debate on the relative merits of the two systems is one of the most important economic controversies of the 1990s. The topic is timely, since the financial systems of those countries are in the process of restructuring. We find that the experience of the emerging stock markets confirms much of the analysis of the benefits of stock markets discussed in the previous chapters.

In the former centrally planned economies, much work remains to be done before the full benefit of a financial system can be realized. Their financial markets cannot yet fulfil their functions with full effectiveness, since some basic prerequisites are lacking. Among them are the incompletely developed legal structure of property rights and "market economy ethos," the limited range of available savings instruments, and the prevailing negative real rate of return on savings. Such structural and institutional weaknesses, coupled in most of these countries with budgetary deficits and high rates of inflation, have so far curtailed the impact of the stock market on economic development (Calvo and Kumar, 1993, p. 6). The lessons learned in our analysis of the Canadian stock market suggest that there is hope for these economies, once some of these defects are rectified.

The "emerging markets" in newly industrialized countries in Asia and elsewhere and in some developing countries have exhibited remarkable rates of growth. One of their weaknesses tends to be high volatility, caused in part by high concentration of share ownership and thinness of trading. The relative importance of equity markets as a source of business financing in these countries is, however, many times greater in relative terms than is the case in the developed industrialized countries.

We first discuss the development of capital markets in the former centrally planned economies, together with the various forms and methods of privatization of state-owned enterprises, and review the trading practices and trends on selected stock exchanges in central and eastern European countries. This analysis provides a perspective on the progress made to date. Next, we summarize the debate on the respective roles banks and stock markets should play in the process of privatization and economic restructuring, with specific reference to the individual emerging economies. We conclude with observations on equity markets as a source of business financing in different types of economies. We show that the potential benefits of stock markets depend in large part on the extent to which the underlying economies have developed.

Privatization and capital markets

The most important rationale for privatization of state-owned enterprises in the former centrally planned economies is that of improved efficiency. In addition to privatization, better performance and improved efficiency require several changes in the incentives facing management: first, demonopolization of the product markets, removal of preferences for government-owned firms, and reduction of tariff protection; second, introduction of a realistic takeover threat into the relationship between managers (agents) and the owners (principals) of the newly privatized industries; and, third, a paradigm shift in organizational culture away from concern with rules and processes, characteristic of the public sector, towards emphasis on outcomes and financial results.

A well-functioning stock market plays a key role in enabling all three types of environmental change. First, as discussed in chapter 3, stock markets are the very mechanism through which takeover threats are implemented. Second, the stock market's "voting booth" function provides an opportunity for investors to evaluate outcomes and financial results of their firms and thus exercise control over management. Finally, stock markets facilitate the formation of capital and the birth of new firms. The entry of new firms contributes to demonopolization of product markets and enhances competition.

An efficient stock market fits importantly into a closely related list of changes in the business environment essential for successful restructuring of these economies. High on the list are macroeconomic stability conducive to private investment; legal and administrative frameworks for private property rights; standards for corporate governance and investor protection; standards of business ethics; agreed accounting systems and conventions; adequate supply of trained accountants, bankers and lawyers; and employment and welfare ("social net") legislation (Parker, 1993).

Methods of privatization

The conversion of state-owned enterprises into privately-owned firms demonstrates yet another aspect of the working of the stock market—the pricing of assets and risks. Pricing is just another term for passing judgment on whether an investment is worthwhile. The stock market cultivates the precision of such judgments. The value of the information generated by trading of claims on assets of the firms being privatized is vividly illustrated by a comparison of the various approaches to privatization. The post-communist governments of eastern and central European countries adopted, in various combinations, the following methods of privatization (Parker, 1993).

Restitution

The most obvious method of privatization is the return of property forcibly seized after the Communist takeover of power in the late 1940s and early 1950s. It requires verification of claims, which tends to slow down the process. The uncertainty of ownership discourages potential investors, and the resulting allocation of productive assets is not necessarily efficient, since those who end up owning them may not be any better managers than were the former communist bureaucrats.

Direct sale to residents

This method has been applied mainly to the sale of small and medium sized businesses, and typically takes the form of an auction. However, much to the dismay of the "ordinary citizens" of these countries, the successful bidders are frequently former communists who enriched themselves under the old regime. There have also been allegations of collusion among buyers to depress prices, and evidence that some purchases were made by foreign investors acting through domestic intermediaries.

Management and worker buyouts

Some firms have been privatized through buyouts by management and workers. In some countries, the potential owners are required to raise sufficient funds to make the purchase; their inability to do so has reduced the scope for this method of privatization.

The voucher method

This scheme, pioneered in the former Czechoslovakia,[52] appears to be the most successful method of privatization, and is an example that western governments should heed. It is a means of spreading the benefits of share ownership among those citizens who would otherwise be unable to afford it. The process began in the winter of 1991-92, when the Czechoslovak Ministry of Finance issued vouchers (or "coupons"). Every adult citizen was entitled to a book of vouchers, available for an amount of money equivalent to about one week's average wage. The sale of vouchers exceeded expectations, with about 75 percent participation of the eligible population.

The vouchers are denominated in points and have been used to bid for shares in the formerly state-owned firms. Frequently, only a part of the equity of each firm is sold through the voucher scheme. The privatization plan, which must be approved by the responsible ministry, may call for the remainder to be sold directly to domestic and foreign investors. Individuals are given a choice between bidding directly for shares of firms or, instead, using their vouchers to buy shares in investment privatization funds (IPFs) which, in turn, buy shares in the privatized firms. The IPFs are investment funds set up either by private individuals or by banks, and are organized as joint stock companies.

Bidding takes place in several rounds and price is adjusted in each round until demand matches supply. When the number of points bid for a firm is insufficient to sell all the shares, another round of bidding is arranged at a reduced price. When the demand for shares exceeds supply, the bids of the IPFs are scaled down, while bids by individuals are met in full. However, when the initial bids exceed supply by 25 percent or more, the points are returned to the voucher holders, and a

---

52 Parker (1993, p. 399) notes that "the only other major example of what is in effect a free distribution of shares...prior to the schemes in central and eastern Europe occurred in the Canadian province of British Columbia". He is referring here to the privatization of the British Columbia Resources Investment Corporation (BCRIC) by the government of Premier W.A.C. Bennett.

new round of bidding is arranged at a higher price. This system is very efficient, as the bidding reflects the knowledge and informed opinion of investors, who separate the strong prospects from the weak ones.

The voucher scheme has made possible a wide dispersion of share ownership and has facilitated the privatization of large enterprises. It has reduced opposition to privatization by enabling the public to participate in potential future gains. Unlike other methods of privatization, it does not require direct negotiation and detailed valuation of companies. This vastly accelerates the process of privatization, since the standard methods of valuing companies are not applicable, given the unreliability of the balance sheet data inherited from the centrally planned economies. The voucher method acts as a substitute for public flotation of shares in economies where there exist no developed stock markets in which the shares could be traded. One deficiency of the scheme is that no new capital or expertise are injected into the privatized enterprise (unlike in the case of acquisition by foreign investors). It is also possible that many shareholders will sell their equity quickly once regular share trading begins.

The voucher system holds lessons for countries such as Canada that are contemplating privatizing public services, such as the post office and passenger rail service. The bidding process would ensure that fair value were placed on the service (unlike, for example, in the Pearson Airport case), and the vouchers could be used to guarantee a minimum domestic ownership if this were deemed desirable.

Acquisitions by foreign investors

The attitudes to foreign ownership in the former centrally planned economies vary widely. However, the need for capital, new technology, and Western managerial and marketing skills is paramount, and foreign investors have been encouraged to participate in the privatization process by competing in public bids, arranging deals with existing management, and entering into joint ventures. We too in Canada have been leery of foreign investors, especially in such strategic areas as resources and financial services, but perhaps the lessons of eastern Europe should show us that there is no point in rejecting expertise.

Stock market trading in former centrally planned economies

Stock markets in the former centrally planned economies are still in their infancies and information on their performances is quite limited. Below, we offer a brief review of four markets for which data are available. The review suggests that stock markets have become a widely accepted institution and an integral part of the economic system of these countries, although they vary greatly in their breadth, rate of growth, volume of trading, and impact on the economy. Our survey concludes with a brief comparative discussion of the alternative method of financing of capital expansion—the "bank-dominated system."

The Warsaw Stock Exchange

Stock market trading started in April 1991 with stocks of five carefully selected industrial enterprises. By the end of 1992, there were 16 listed companies (EcoDiagnostic, 1993, p. 27). As of November 1993, there were still only 22 stocks traded on the Warsaw Stock Exchange, and the overall market capitalization was around U.S. $2 billion. This amounts to only U.S. $34 per capita, while in the Czech Republic the per capita stock portfolio as of November 1993 was estimated at around U.S. $500, and was expected to increase by 50-75 percent by the spring of 1994. During the first half of 1993, the Polish stock market gained 213 percent in U.S. dollar terms. This was the best performance anywhere in the world. The second highest performer, the Turkish stock market, gained "only" 114 percent over the same period (PlanEcon, 1993, pp. 1-2).

The Budapest Stock Exchange

The Hungarian stock market (consisting of 25 stocks traded on the Budapest Stock Exchange) was established in June 1990. In contrast to the Polish stock market, it declined by 16 percent in dollar terms during the first half of 1993. It did, however, stage a rally, and between June 30 and November 5 was among the top five performers among the emerging markets.

Several factors suggest that the future potential of the Hungarian stock market is considerable. First, the price-earnings ratios in November 1993 were in the range of 12-14, compared with over 18 in Poland. The implication of a lower price-earnings ratio is that investors can still get a bargain compared to a higher priced market. Second, the Hungarian population has not as yet acquired a taste for stock market investments. Third, one of the political objectives of the Hungarian government is to create a broad base of shareholding among the domestic population. It is therefore likely to accelerate the flow of initial public offerings which will stimulate the market activity (PlanEcon, 1993, p. 3).

The Czech and Slovak Stock Markets

The Czech stock market effectively started operating on June 22, 1993, roughly two years later than the Polish and Hungarian markets. Despite its relatively short existence, it has been recently characterized as "an experiment unlike anything seen in any other emerging market" (PlanEcon, 1993, p. 3). It grew out of the voucher method of privatization of almost 1,000 companies whose shares now trade on two markets: the Prague Stock Exchange, and the electronic RM-System (over-the-counter market). As of November 1993, only 20-50 issues have traded actively, and only three (all banks) have been listed on the exchange. The other issues have been unlisted, but some of them were expected to become listed stocks (PlanEcon, 1993, p. 22).

The volume of trading was initially very small, in part because most stocks were initially quoted at unrealistically high levels and were not traded while the markets searched for prices which made sense. These were reached in late August and early September of 1993, and since that time volumes have been growing, partly because Western portfolio investors have been buying substantial numbers of shares in the most attractive privatized companies.

A recent report by Deutsche Bank predicts that between 6 and 25 percent of Czech investors will claim their profits from investments in the investment funds (there were 353 investment funds in the Czech Republic as of December 1993). Some of them promised, in their advertising, a ten-fold return on vouchers, and if they are to deliver on these promises, they would have to liquidate many of their shareholdings, thus depressing share prices.[53] This could have a dampening effect on the growth of the market as other investors would see their wealth decline and be averse to invest more.

The Slovak economy is smaller and the political competence and commitment of the Slovak government to economic reform much weaker than is the case in the Czech Republic. For these reasons, the Slovak stocks are generally cheaper than stocks on the Prague Stock Exchange. However, a number of Slovak companies are technologically advanced and successful in the export markets. They do, therefore, have considerable growth potential.

The Russian Stock Market

The Russian government issued free vouchers to 140 million citizens in 1992, to buy shares in some 10,000 companies up for sale, representing half of Russia's industrial capital. The face value of each voucher was 10,000 rubles (worth about $25 U.S. at the end of 1992). In April 1993, the vouchers were selling in the secondary market for only 4,500 rubles, since most Russians assumed that privatization would not take place and vouchers would be worthless. This opinion changed when, in July 1993, the government ordered state firms to auction off a minimum 29 percent stake to the public.

In the aftermath of the December 1993 Russian election success of the anti-reformist party led by Vladimir Zhirinovsky, the price of vouchers fell from the pre-election level of 24,000 rubles to between 18,200 and 20,000 rubles (about $16 U.S.) on the Moscow and St. Petersburg exchanges. This is a clear sign of the effect that political uncertainty can have on the creation of wealth. At the end of 1993, more than 55 million Russians owned shares in some type of business. About 70 percent of small and medium-sized enterprises have been privatized, and 11,000 of the 14,000 large enterprises to be privatized have been transformed into joint stock companies.[54]

---

53 *The Economist*, December 11, 1993, p. 91.

54 The previous three paragraphs draw on the following sources: "Russian stock exchange functions without stocks," Toronto *Star*, August 22, 1993,

This market is still in the early stages of its development; there is no trading of stocks to speak of, but there exists active trade in privatization vouchers. Measured in dollar terms, the vouchers' free market price has more than quadrupled between April and November 1993 (PlanEcon, 1993, p. 5).

While the supply of vouchers is large, the equity market is illiquid. That is, there are few investors ready to produce money for new projects. One reason is that firms are only obliged to offer 30 percent of their shares as voucher options, and the rest are acquired by workers or managers or kept by the government, none of whom brings in new money. The other reason is that company managers have no incentive to encourage buying and selling of shares, since they have to offer shares to investors in exchange for vouchers, and thus receive no capital. To maintain the status quo and to protect their position from the discontent of shareholders (especially large ones), they have resorted to a variety of tactics, including "physically threatening challengers at shareholder meetings, rigging votes, and refusing to record trends in corporate share registers."[55]

This approach to privatization resulted in managers and workers owning an average of 70 percent of all privatized companies. Because of the managers' influence over workers, there has developed "an alliance of managers and workers which is unique to Russia ... managers are emerging from privatization with often quite substantial ownership of cashflows . . . [and] tremendous amounts of control."[56]

---

p. H1; "Russian vouchers: Further to rise," *The Economist*, November 13, 1993, p. 90; "Zhirinovsky jitters jolt Russian markets", The *Globe and Mail*, December 16, 1993, p. B9A; "Russian people flock to buy shares", The *Globe and Mail*, December 30, 1993, p. B7.

55 "High stakes on the high steppe," *The Economist*, October 16, 1993, p. 90.

56 "Can they make a democracy?" *The Economist*, October 2, 1993, pp. 21-23.

Limitations of stock markets in former centrally planned economies

In the absence of institutions such as investment funds (as we see in the Czech Republic), the voucher scheme of privatization promotes widely dispersed share ownership, which may lead to a weakening of shareholder control over management. This is the case when an individual shareholder's cost of monitoring corporate performance and the cost of trading in shares exceed the benefits. Such benefit-cost comparisons are more favourable—and the shareholder control over management stronger—when institutions such as investment privatization funds (IPFs) are the major shareholders. However, some countries have enacted legislation limiting the size of an IPF's holdings in any one company, supposedly in the interest of promoting competition.[57] Privatization programs with such limitations are thus creating an ownership structure of the "Anglo-Saxon," rather than of the European-Japanese type (Parker, 1993, p. 400).

Some sceptics among the Western experts on eastern Europe believe that the idea that the stock exchange will play a big role in corporate finance is "an illusion." Most firms will have to depend on banks, presumably even if the development of stock markets is afforded a priority.[58] This view is questionable on theoretical grounds; in addition, in the present state, the banking system in the transition economies is not up to the task.

Theoretical analysis highlights the advantages of stock markets in conditions of lack of consensus on how production should be organized and thus disagreement on how firms should be run. The markets repeatedly evaluate the relationship between actions of firms and their outcomes and work best in industries which are somewhat less competitive, or where there is a lag between actions and outcomes, or where technology is changing. Allen (1993) cites the importance of the stock

---

57 The Czechoslovak legislation, for example, restricted an IPF's holding in any one company to 20 percent (Parker, 1993, p. 400).

58 "One little piggy went to market—but starved," *The Economist*, November 27, 1993, p. 84.

market in the U.K. during the 19th century when it was the first country to experience the industrial revolution, or the heavy reliance on the stock market in the U.S. as the first country to enter the post-industrial society. In some respects, the transition economies are in a somewhat similar situation; stock markets, therefore, should have an important role to play.

The banking sector in most of the transition economies is characterized by structural weakness due to inadequate accounting and auditing procedures, and large non-performing loans on the balance sheets. Bank personnel have relatively little experience in the business of financial intermediation and have limited ability to assess and manage risks, to plan and control profit, to develop management information systems, and to budget and manage performance (Catte and Mastropasqua, 1993; Miurin and Sommariva, 1993). Both the structural weaknesses and the inability of banks to provide adequate corporate governance suggest that "the authorities cannot rely at the early period of transition on banks to exert direct or indirect control on enterprises" (Thorne, 1993, p. 998).

Banks or equity markets?

During the 1970s and 1980s, the role of capital markets in the OECD countries has increased, while the contribution of banks has diminished. The emergence of stock markets in many developing countries suggests that similar trends are taking place in those economies as well (EcoDiagnostic, 1993, p. 4).

The former centrally planned economies can derive three main benefits from the development of equity markets: the provision of long-term risk capital and diversification of risks; investor control over the management of firms; and supply of foreign portfolio investment (Calvo and Kumar, 1993, pp. 17-19). The importance of equity markets as a source of long-term risk capital rises in a climate of economic instability, characteristic of transitional stages of economic development. Firms may not be able to obtain adequate funds for potentially profitable investment opportunities with uncertain payoffs, since banks tend to prefer well-established, safe borrowers.

One possible remedy is for regulations to allow the banks to be direct participants in the process of restructuring the creditor firms. In the context of the former centrally planned economies, this is an appealing suggestion, for several reasons. First, banks are the only part of the existing financial system capable of absorbing a large amount of equity; second, they are among the few existing institutions (together with the investment privatization funds) that could provide corporate governance; third, a close financial relationship between banks and industrial firms (of the type common in continental Europe and Japan) is beneficial when financial markets are underdeveloped; and, fourth, in many advanced economies, banks do hold large portion of the equity of industrial firms.

However, the financial instability which will likely accompany the transition to a market economy could jeopardize the financial position of banks holding a large amount of equity. The banks could also be in a position of conflict of interest if they are both owners and creditors of firms that should be closed down as a part of the process of restructuring (Calvo and Kumar, 1993, p. 19).

Capital markets provide an alternative and a necessary complement to the banking system, since they make it possible for firms to issue equity to the public and thus spread risks among a large number of investors (shareholders). The investors, in turn, can diversify their risks by buying shares of different firms in a variety of industries.

The role of stock markets as a means of investor control over management has been alluded to in several previous chapters. In chapter 3, we focused on mergers and takeovers as a vehicle for asserting this control. This function takes on added importance both in the former centrally planned and in developing economies where management is a scarce resource and the efficiency of its allocation has significant payoffs.

Finally, the development of stock markets in the former centrally planned economies has opened up new opportunities for Western institutional investors to diversify their assets geographically. Based on the analysis of the 1993 trends in these markets, the expected returns on investment in most of these markets for 1994 and beyond appear excellent and should attract significant amounts of foreign capital (PlanEcon, 1993).

One of the weaknesses inherited from the centrally planned economic system is the absence of reliable valuation of assets. No one really knows what the old state companies are worth. It has slowed down the process of privatization, since governments are reluctant to "sell off national assets too cheaply." A functioning stock market is the only institution capable of assessing the value of assets on the basis of prevailing macroeconomic conditions and investors' evaluation of the firms' prospects (EcoDiagnostic, 1993, p. 29).

Other "emerging markets"

The recent experience of the "emerging markets" in developing and newly industrialized countries may offer some insight into the longer-term growth prospects for the stock markets in the former centrally planned economies. These equity markets have grown extremely fast and their capitalization (the total value of the shares outstanding) exceeds the market capitalization in several developed countries. For example, in Korea the market capitalization grew from six percent of GNP in 1980 to over 80 percent by the end of 1990, which represents a 40-fold increase in market volume. In India, over the four-year period ending in 1990, the market capitalization grew from four to nine percent of GNP. In these two countries, the capital market accounted for about 15 percent of all sources of financing for gross asset formation during the period 1980-1987 (Calvo and Kumar, 1993, p. 18).

Western mutual funds investing in the emerging markets have experienced a boom, since investors anticipate that the equity values in developing countries should rise more rapidly than in mature economies. For example, the Investment Funds Institute of Canada reported that gross sales of foreign bond and income funds in the nine months ending in September 1993 were up 311 percent compared with the corresponding period of 1992. This increase is reflected in growing geographic diversity of Canadian investments. As an illustration, Templeton Management Ltd. traded with just eight offshore exchanges in

Table 7: Sources of Funds of Nonfinancial Enterprises in Large Industrialized Countries, 1970-85 (Percent of net investment expenditure)

Source	Canada	France	Germany	Italy	Japan	U.K.	U.S.
Internal	76.4	61.4	70.9	51.9	59.9	102.4	85.9
External	23.6	38.6	29.1	48.1	42.1	-2.4	14.1
Of Which							
Loans	15.2	37.3	12.1	27.7	50.4	7.6	24.4
Trade Credit	-4.4	-0.6	-2.1	—	-11.2	-1.1	-1.4
Bonds	8.5	1.6	-1.0	1.6	2.1	-1.1	11.6
Short-Term Sec.	-0.6	-0.1	-0.1	-1.3	—	1.7	0.4
Equities	2.5	6.3	0.6	8.2	4.6	-3.3	1.1
Other	-2.4	-5.8	19.5	11.9	-3.8	-6.1	-22.0

Source: Calvo and Kumar (1993), p. 30.

1981, but in 1993 it conducted research on 42 exchanges, and was expecting to deal with 60 or more exchanges by the end of the century.[59]

The importance of the emerging markets to their countries is best illustrated by comparing the structure of the sources of business financing in the developing and newly industrialized countries with the structure in industrialized countries. One type of comparison can be made at the "microeconomic," or company level. It is clear that nonfinancial corporations in the seven largest industrialized countries rely primarily on internal sources for financing of corporate growth. Table 7 gives the distribution of sources of funds used by the corporate sector, averaged over the period 1970 to 1985, broken down into internal funds (retentions) and external funds. The data are reported on a net basis, (i.e.

---

59 "Stock markets spring up after Communism's demise," The *Globe and Mail*, November 23, 1993, p. C2.

they exclude corporate deposits to banks and equities redeemed during the period). The table shows that retained profits accounted for more than 100 percent of finance for all nonfinancial corporations in the U.K., over 85 percent in the U.S., and just over one half in Italy.

Only a small share of funds is raised in the securities markets, and the share of equity markets is lower than five percent in all countries except France and Italy. Bank loans are important, especially in France, Italy, and Japan. One explanation for the dominance of internal financing is that external investors or creditors find it costly to intervene in management. The shares of internal financing are especially high in countries where the separation between management and the sources of financing is the most pronounced, i.e. the U.K., U.S., and Canada. In countries such as Japan, France, and Italy, the financial intermediaries are more closely integrated with the industrial sector. This results in a relatively high share of banks loans among the sources of business financing.

The structure of corporate financing is strikingly different in many newly industrialized and developing countries. Table 8 is based on the company accounts of the top 50 manufacturing companies quoted on the stock market of each country. For this sample, the reliance on external finance is much greater than in the industrialized countries. For example, external financing exceeded 80 percent of net investment expenditures in Jordan and Turkey, came close to that level in Korea and Thailand, and averaged around 60 percent in all other countries, except Malaysia. In more than half of the countries in the table, the companies used much more equity than debt to finance their growth.

However, the absolute amounts invested in the emerging stock markets are much lower than in the developed industrialized countries. Thus, a "macroeconomic" comparison, based on the ratio of stock market capitalization to the country's GDP (average for the period 1981-1991), reported in the last column of table 8, suggests that the emerging stock markets play a much more modest role in their economies.[60] With some exceptions, such as Malaysia with stock market

---

60 The ratios reported in table 8 represent averages over a decade. To the extent stock market cycles and business cycles are not synchronized across

Table 8: Sources of Funds of Nonfinancial Enterprises in Selected Developing Countries, 1980-88 (Percentages of net investment expenditures)

Country	Internal Financing	External Financing			Capital as a % of GDP
		Total	Equity	Debt	
India	34.9	65.1	14.0	51.1	7.4
Jordan	11.6	88.4	46.6	41.8	52.4
Korea	21.0	79.0	44.3	34.6	24.8
Malaysia	66.8	33.2	14.9	18.3	75.0
Mexico	26.3	73.7	69.4	4.3	8.1
Pakistan	42.0	58.0	20.4	37.6	6.2
Thailand	24.1	75.9	40.9	35.0	14.4
Turkey	17.5	82.6	60.9	21.7	N.A.
Zimbabwe	42.9	57.1	35.2	21.9	13.7

Sources: Calvo and Kumar (1993), p. 30; EcoDiagnostic (1993), p. 7 for data on "Capitalization as % of GDP."
Note: The data on "Capitalization as % of GDP" is the average for the period 1981-1991, except for Zimbabwe, which is for the period 1982-1991.

capitalization equal to 75 percent of GDP, Jordan, with over 52 percent, and Korea, with almost 25 percent, these ratios for most countries are relatively low. By contrast, the average ratio for the period 1981-1991 for the United Kingdom and Switzerland was around 70 percent. The U.S. ratio was over 50 percent, and in France and Germany it averaged just under 20 percent. In Japan, for the period 1990-1991, it reached almost 90 percent (EcoDiagnostic, 1993, p. 6).

The share of equity markets in the sources of funds used by the corporate sector is, of course, not an adequate measure of their importance. The point has been made that "although from the point of view of

---

the sample countries, the inter-country comparability may be impaired.

Table 9: Equity Market Concentration in Industrialized Countries, End of 1990 (Percent of total)

Country	Share Of Total Market Capitalization Held By Ten Largest Stocks
Canada	28.4
France	25.8
Germany	41.7
Japan	17.1
Switzerland	49.6
United Kingdom	24.4
United States	14.1

Source: Calvo and Kumar (1993), p. 31.

companies, stock markets are insignificant, their impact on the distribution of financial flows within the economy is considerable" (EcoDiagnostic, 1993, p. 2). This is due in part to the role that markets play in financing very large companies, which have a disproportionate impact on the economy.

The concentration of equity holdings, as measured by the share of total market capitalization held by the ten largest stocks, tends to be lower in the industrialized countries. As shown in table 9, it ranged from the low of 14.1 percent in the U.S. to the high of 49.6 percent in Switzerland. Other things equal, lower concentration reduces the volatility of the stock prices traded on the given market.

By contrast, at the same period (end of 1990) developing countries reported ratios as high as 76.9 percent for Colombia, 67.2 percent for Jordan, 61.7 percent for Turkey, etc. In some emerging markets, however, the concentration was much lower, for example 22.4 percent in Brazil, 23.5 percent in India, 25.5 percent in Pakistan, 28.0 percent in Malaysia, 30.9 percent in Korea, etc. (Calvo and Kumar, 1993, p. 31).

The emerging markets have exhibited, especially during the last few years, growth in capitalization many times faster than the rest of the world. Table 10 compares the market capitalization, in billions of U.S. dollars, as of September 30, 1988, and on the same date in 1993. The world-wide capitalization was 1.5 times larger at the end of the five-year period, the U.S. capitalization was 1.7 times larger, and the Japanese market capitalization grew by a mere 2.5 percent. During the same

Table 10: Market Capitalization, Selected Countries, September 30, 1988 and 1993 (Billions of U.S. $)

	September 30, 1988	September 30, 1993
World Index	4,766	7,134
United States	1,468	2,485
Japan	1,881	1,929
Malaysia	15	76
Singapore (Free)	15	50
Thailand	6	27
Indonesia	0.1	10
Philippines (Free)	1	9

Source: "Chasing baby dragons," *The Economist*, October 23, 1993, p. 100.

period the market capitalization in Indonesia increased 100 times, in the Philippines nine times, in Malaysia five times, in Thailand 4.5 times, and in Singapore 3.3 times.

In countries where a large proportion of cash circulates outside the banking system, a part of it tends to be hoarded (temporarily withdrawn from circulation in the form of idle savings). If a stock market is established, it contributes to economic growth by attracting some of the hoarded funds back into circulation and thus increasing the financing capacity of the economy. In addition, access to the stock market enables listed companies to reduce their debt-to-equity ratio and hence makes them better risks for the banking system. Banks can then lend to other borrowers on more generous terms.

If, however, securities are purchased with funds previously entrusted to the banking system, total bank deposits are lowered, forcing the banks to cut back on their lending. This response reduces the financing capacity of the banking system.

The net impact of these contradictory influences on the economies of developing countries is uncertain. Stock markets have been an important and growing but still relatively small part of the development of emerging economies. These countries have much still to learn from us, as do we from them (as in the example of the Czech voucher system of privatization).

Conclusion

In this chapter, we first discussed the actual and potential role of the stock market in the former centrally planned economies. We noted the rapid, but as yet incomplete, evolution of institutional and legal prerequisites for an effective functioning of the markets. Among the various approaches to re-establishment of private ownership of assets, the voucher method appears to be the most successful, and represents a means of spreading the benefits of share ownership to a large number of citizens.

Our conclusion is that the prospects for a reasonably rapid development of a full-fledged financial system and stock market mechanism are uneven, with countries like the Czech and Slovak Republics, Poland and Hungary being closest to this objective, Russia lagging somewhat behind, and most of the others merely in initial stages. We also reviewed the ways in which the various stock exchanges function and summarized the information on their—generally promising—short- and near-term potential.

Banks frequently act as lenders preferring well-established, safe borrowers. Equity markets therefore have an advantage as a source of long-term risk financing in a climate of economic instability characteristic of transitional economies. They complement the banking system by making it possible to capitalize firms publicly and offering investors the opportunity to diversify their risks. The ability to diversify risk, of course, also encourages risk taking.

The takeover threat exercised through the stock market helps influence management behaviour. This function assumes considerable importance in transition economies where management is a scarce resource. Reallocation of management resources across firms can, therefore, have a high potential payoff.

We concluded the chapter with a statistical overview of the recent experience of the "emerging markets" in developing and newly industrialized countries. It showed that, at the macro level, the capitalization of the emerging markets is small, both in absolute terms and as a percentage of GDP. However, business firms in these countries rely on stock markets as a source of financing to a much greater degree than firms in developed industrialized countries. Our review of the relevant literature suggests that the impact of the emerging stock markets on the distribution of financial flows and on the structure of their economies is considerable.

We tend to take the features of our developed economy for granted. Through analyzing the laboratory of nascent economies such as those in eastern Europe, we are able to reflect on what works well in our economy and what does not. The economic development role being played by the stock market in these economies gives perspective on the role played by the market in Canada. At the same time, the privatization role of the stock market in these economies provides guidance for us as to the potential role of the Canadian market in privatizing Canadian public services.

Chapter 6: Ethical Issues

(or "How Much Can One Get Away With in the Stock Market?")

Introduction

THE PREVIOUS CHAPTERS ANALYZED THE activities of the stock market with emphasis on its contribution to the efficient allocation of resources. Specifically, we dealt with the market's role as a link between investors (savers) and entrepreneurs, and defined the various types of efficiency promoted through the workings of the stock market. Next, we discussed mergers and takeovers as a mechanism through which shareholders assert their control over managers, and commented on the crucial role of evolving stock markets in the former centrally planned economies of central and eastern Europe in their transition to full-fledged market economies.

In this chapter, we draw upon the business ethics literature to assess two areas of the functioning of the stock market. First, we consider the ethical issues in mergers and takeovers. We focus on the various defensive measures taken by management of the target companies and show how they undermine the social benefits of the stock market. Second, we review the controversy on the moral defensibility of the practice of "insider trading," much debated in the press, and highlight the tenuous nature of the arguments for its regulation.

The dominant theme of this chapter is that takeover threats and stock market transactions, together with the rules of behaviour given by the "loyal agent" concept (discussed below) force managers to act ethically, i.e. in the interest of shareholders. Stock markets are populated by a large number of buyers and sellers and, as discussed in chapter 4, absorb and process information with considerable efficiency. Because of these features, they come quite close to the economics textbooks' definition of the "competitive market." In a functioning competitive market, no one buyer or seller can significantly influence the price or any other terms. Individual market participants cannot, therefore, deliberately exercise any "social responsibility" or obligation to sacrifice their own good for the benefit of the society at large, other than the duty to obey the law (Friedman, 1962). The enforcement of social interests rests, in a large part, with the market.

Takeover transactions described in chapter 3—and more generally the stock market acting as a "giant voting booth"—are crucial components of the market for corporate control which replaces managers who fall short of their mandate. A recent example is the Royal Oak Mines attempt to buy Lac Minerals, where Royal Oak Chairperson Margaret Witte has claimed that Lac management has been wasteful with their operating expenditures. She claims to be able to trim millions of dollars a year by selling the corporate jet, closing the "opulent" head office, and reducing the number of managers.

The media periodically raise concerns about the ethics of the activities of the various actors directly involved in the day-to-day working of the stock market, including investment dealers, underwriters, brokers, and floor traders. The history of the stock market experience in many countries abounds with examples of questionable practices in this segment of the securities industry, and the resulting close attention paid to them by government regulators. We deal with some of these issues and regulatory responses in chapter 7, "Whither Regulation?"

The distinction between the interests of shareholders and the interests of managers is an important aspect of the application of ethical concepts to the area of corporate decision making, including the participation of business firms in the activities of the stock market. We therefore begin this chapter with a brief selective summary of the long-standing debate on "corporate social responsibility" and show the key role of the stock market in enforcing the performance of management's duties toward shareholders. We then proceed to discuss the weaknesses in the various defences against takeovers and leveraged buyouts, and conclude with an evaluation of insider trading and the controversy surrounding its regulation.

Ethical concepts in corporate decision making

The ethics of management behaviour should be judged by its consistency with the interests of shareholders. In this section, we briefly discuss the limits on management loyalty to shareholders, and some aspects of the distinction between the actions of corporations and actions of human persons.

Executive officers of a corporation are usually elected by the shareholders (or appointed by shareholder representatives). Following a well-known economic view of a corporation (Friedman, 1962), shareholders are capable of deciding whether the corporation will behave in a "socially responsible way," for example, whether it will make charitable donations. The executive officers have a responsibility to pursue the interests of shareholders, within the rights and duties of the corporation. Decisions regarding "socially responsible" or "charitable" behaviour of the corporation cannot therefore be left to the executive officers, but must be made by shareholders. These types of behaviours can, of course, be motivated by managers' desires to improve the corporate image or the loyalty of the corporation's employees. In such cases, these decisions are merely good business practice, and not a demonstration that the corporation possesses some kind of "moral virtue."

Corporations are legal persons (entities with rights and duties before the law), and as such can act justly or unjustly. It is less clear, however, whether the behaviour of corporations can be judged by the standards normally applied to human persons—for example, whether they can be said to have virtues and vices, such as generosity, courage, meanness or cowardice. Virtues "are a matter of caring about certain sorts of things" (Ewin, 1991, p. 752), but the corporation, as distinct from its representatives, does not care about its interests. The interests of a corporation are determined by the purpose for which it was formed. It may be to maximize the returns to its shareholders, but (as in the case of corporations formed for charitable purposes) the objective could also be to raise and distribute the largest possible amount of money for a particular cause.

We take the view that managers are required to act as representatives of owners; if they deviate from the objective of the corporation, they can be said to have failed in their duty. There are, however, limits to the manager's duties which arise from our legal and social institutions. Specifically, the rules of agency, as commonly understood, stipulate that by agreeing to serve as someone's agent, a person accepts a legal (and moral) duty to serve the client loyally, obediently, and in a confidential manner. But in determining whether the orders of the client (or of the employer(s), or representative(s) of shareholders) are reasonable, the agent must consider business or professional ethics, and in no way has a duty to perform acts which are illegal or unethical. Put another way, an agreement to serve other people does not automatically justify doing wrong on their behalf.

Debate on the ethics of takeovers

The periodic waves of corporate mergers and takeovers have been the subject of considerable attention in the media, much of it in the form of attacks on "corporate greed." Unfortunately, the contribution of mergers and takeovers to economic efficiency and competitiveness is much too often disregarded or underplayed. In what follows, we review the main objections to takeovers, and their weaknesses, from the perspective of economic efficiency.

A major target of criticism is takeovers initiated for the purpose of liquidating the target company. This occurs in situations where there is a significant gap between the market value and the breakup value of the company assets. If the incumbent management is unable or unwilling to close the gap by changing its practices, an outside bidder (or in the emotionally charged language of the media, a "corporate raider" or a "shark")[61] offers to buy a significant percentage of the company shares from other shareholders at prices exceeding the current market value. If successful, the bidder buys the company, and sells off the underlying assets at a profit.

The usual objections against the practice of breaking up and selling off parts of the purchased company ("liquidating buyouts") fall into three categories (Almeder and Carey, 1991).

1. Liquidating buyouts have a negative effect on some individuals and groups

This objection is directed at buyouts of companies that are profitable and whose employees are, by implication, not obviously incompetent. The buyouts may lead to layoffs and changes in management ranks and have a variety of negative effects on the community where the company is located. Critics assert that "the pleasure and limited good of a few" derived from enlarging the pre-takeover profit cannot be justified by "the overwhelming human suffering typically involved when a large company is liquidated" (Almeder and Carey, 1991, p. 472).

The basis of such criticism seems to be the belief that the increased profits are the result of wealth transfers, rather than long-term efficiency improvements brought about by the merger. The immediate consequence of layoffs may indeed be a reduction or loss of income for some individuals. However, policies restricting or preventing takeovers would induce investors to take their capital elsewhere and eventually lead to the decline of the firm and reduction in the efficiency of the economy.

It is legitimate to ask in this context why the good of the shareholders should be dominant in determining the responsibilities of managers—why not also the good of the workers, the community where the plant is located, or the society at large? The experience of centrally-planned economies and other bureaucratized systems provides a rather convincing answer: asking managers to maximize some measure of

---

61 Based on the pejorative characterization of the bidding firm as a "shark," the anti-takeover defences are sometimes described as "shark repellents."

total social goodness, while superficially appealing, does not deliver the right amount of goods at the right time and place, and at the right price. The excessively broad definition of managerial duties was one of the sources of the failure of that system.

Utilitarian ethics postulates that human actions are to be judged by their consequences—in this case by their contribution to economic prosperity—and provides a justification for narrowing of the focus of managerial responsibility. Shareholder profits are relatively easy to measure; this is one of the advantages of using them as a criterion of management performance. A structure of incentives based on profits is logical and minimizes the need for information. Takeover threats and stock market responses to management performance are a part of this system of incentives (Sen, 1993, p. 219).

2. The "neglect of long-term investments" (once again)

Critics contend that the threat of corporate takeover compels managers to show evidence of continuous profitability and avoid long-term investments (e.g., in R&D). This pressure allegedly undermines long-term capital formation and competitiveness of the economy. A special target of such criticism appear to be liquidating buyouts.

As discussed in chapter 3, neither the U.S. nor the Canadian empirical evidence supports the view that mergers, or the threat of takeovers, diminish long-term investment in R&D. Moreover, the fact that buyers are able to make a profit on liquidating buyouts suggests that the utilization of the assets of the target companies by the pre-takeover management left something to be desired. Once again, advocacy of restrictions on such buyouts on "ethical grounds" may lead to unethical results; regulations forbidding the new owners to break up the company might prevent them from remedying the mistakes of the previous managers.

3. Moral duties associated with ownership

Buyouts followed by break-up and sale of parts of the firm are sometimes viewed as an attack on the right of ownership (Almeder and

Carey, 1991, p. 474). Institutional investors are singled out for a particular criticism on the grounds that they have only limited interest in the preservation of the existing companies "for future growth." However, the paramount social interest in producing long-term wealth requires that the right to private ownership and its free exercise not be restricted, except to protect society against practices which are shown to cause net long-term harm. In the case of takeovers and liquidating buyouts, much of the evidence summarized in chapter 3 supports the view that they promote efficient re-allocation of capital. The opposition of the target company management is motivated largely by the self-interest of incumbents.

It is of course possible that the bidder makes a mistake in attempting a liquidating takeover, and the management of the target firm should be permitted to defend the corporation. A successful defence requires a demonstration that the apparent inefficiency of the target corporation—manifest in the excess of breakup value of assets over market value—is only temporary, and that the preservation of the integrity of existing assets is in the long-term interest of shareholders. Anti-takeover defences are ethically permissible only if they have the support of the majority of the target company shareholders (Almeder and Carey, 1991, p. 480).

Leveraged management buyouts

Leveraged buyouts of firms by their own managers have been subject not only to critical scrutiny, but also to calls for outright prohibition. We believe that one should distinguish between two types of situations. First, there may be cases where managers manipulate the firm's earnings downward prior to the bid in order to reduce the buyout price to themselves. This occurs at the expense of shareholders, and should be dealt with as a violation of the fiduciary duty of managers.

A second, and more subtle, concern arises from the asymmetry of knowledge: Only the managers know what the value of the firm would be if some of its assets were sold off. Since this superior knowledge constitutes inside information, critics have argued that management buyouts violate the prohibition on insider trading, as well as the disclosure rules of the securities regulations because managers do not disclose that the firm is worth more than their bid (Jones and Hunt, 1991, p. 835).

In our view, regulatory restrictions on management buyouts are unnecessary and damaging in the long run. Management bids for shares of their own firm will be observed by other potential investors and taken as a signal that the firm is undervalued. This point is quite general and is well known in economics, at least since Hayek's (1945) development of the argument; market participants develop an understanding of the relationship between prices and privately held information. Thus, even traders who do not have access to private information will be able to infer something about its content from the movements of the current market price. The stock market makes it possible both for existing shareholders and for new investors to participate in the gains from changing ownership structure. These gains would not occur if management buyouts were prohibited.

The consequences of the informational asymmetry between managers and outsiders could be mitigated if it were possible to establish, in advance, a "fair" price for the company's shares. One definition of fairness is a "synthetic standard" price, established by estimating the value that shareholders could obtain if they synthesized the buyout on their own.

A group of shareholders could "synthetize" the buyout if they borrowed money, repurchased a large percentage of shares, and increased the share ownership of managers. The increase in the value of the firm resulting from these actions would accrue to shareholders. The magnitude of this increase therefore represents a starting point for buyout negotiations between managers and the board of directors (Jones and Hunt, 1991, p. 836).

The ethics of management defence against takeovers

Methods of defence

The managers of target companies have at their disposal numerous techniques and practices which could be used to ward off a potential takeover threat. Some of them have been discussed in previous chapters.

A fairly complete list includes the following: The "poison pill"; issuing a large block of new common stock; supermajority requirements; staggered board terms (classified boards of directors); noncumulative voting; the issuance of two-class common stock; the "scorched earth" tactic; and the "premium-price selective buyback" (Almeder and Carey, 1991, pp. 480-482; Meade and Davidson, 1993, pp. 90-91). In this section, we briefly outline the mechanics of some of these defences and show that their success in many cases depends on the passivity of shareholders or their unwillingness to incur costs in protecting their interests.

The "poison pill" may take the form of a new issue of preferred stock[62] of the target company which the management distributes to the existing shareholders. If the takeover succeeds, the holders of preferred shares have the option to buy shares of the acquired company at a discount—sometimes as much as 50 percent of its market price. This makes the takeover very costly to the acquirer. If the poison pill is in place before a specific bid is made, the bidder is likely to offer a lower price and the takeover may not succeed.

The distribution of preferred shares is welcome news to those recipients who have a vested interest in preservation of the existing management. Other shareholders, however, may not approve of the management tactics and may fight the poison pill in shareholder meetings and in the courts. This was the case, for example, in late 1988 when the management of Inco, concerned with a potential takeover, proposed and implemented a special cash dividend payment and a plan to increase the number of outstanding shares in the event of a takeover. In this instance, the minority shareholders were unsuccessful and the poison pill remained in place.

Supermajority requirements are amendments to company bylaws which stipulate that a merger, or sale of assets, or other specified transactions must be approved by substantially more than 50 percent of shareholder votes. The required majority level often exceeds the normal

---

62 Preferred stock is a security (usually non-voting) with a claim on assets and income of the corporation which ranks higher than the claim of common stocks, but lower than debt instruments.

shareholder participation at meetings, which makes it virtually impossible to approve a merger.

In principle, shareholders could join together and defeat such amendments by means of proxy voting and similar actions. In practice, however, a typical small shareholder is not prepared to organize a concerted action, since the share of the total benefits accruing to an individual shareholders is quite small, while the costs borne by the individual may be substantial. The weakening of shareholder rights resulting from the presence of supermajority requirements should, in theory, be reflected in a lower market price of the stock. In practice, however, it is unlikely that most investors consider such factors in their decision to purchase the stock.

Similar considerations apply with respect to shareholder reactions to a takeover defence in the form of staggered terms for members of the board of directors. The consequence of this arrangement is that only a fraction (one half or one third) of the board members are eligible for election each year. This prevents the acquiring company from taking control of the board until at least two regular board elections have been held.

Some companies have implemented cumulative voting procedures to allow minority groups representation on the board of directors. Each shareholder has votes equal to the number of his or her shares times the number of directors to be elected, and the shareholder is allowed to cast all of those votes for a single director. Noncumulative voting, by contrast, enforces the "one share one vote" rule and thus confers an advantage on large shareholders. In this sense, it may be interpreted as a takeover defence, since it makes it difficult for small shareholders to concentrate all of their votes for one candidate. A minority shareholder who is also a potential acquirer thus may not be able to get representation on the board of the target company.

Dual class capitalization plans create a second category of common stock, typically giving superior voting rights to long-term (more loyal) stockholders (see our discussion in chapter 2). Another type, called "substantial shareholder provision," reduces the voting power of the holder when a prespecified amount of ownership is reached. In those situations where there exist two classes of common shares, those with the greater voting power are frequently concentrated in the hands of shareholders sympathetic to the incumbent management. As a result, the acquirer faces greater obstacles in assuming control of the target company.

Our observations on the Canadian Tire Corporation in chapter 2 illustrate the point. The Billes family owned 4 percent of the outstanding shares of the company, but commanded 60 percent of the votes. The vast majority of shareholders would clearly have no say in any potential takeover of the corporation.

The "scorched earth" defences include the selling off of desirable assets of the target company, or the reverse, depleting its cash reserves by making extensive (and not necessarily profitable) acquisitions, possibly incurring large debts in the process. While these tactics may protect the management against a takeover, they render the company vulnerable to the vagaries of the business cycle.

In a "premium-price selective buyback," management of the target company offers to buy at a premium all shares except those purchased by the acquiring company.[63] The management is in a position to offer such a premium in anticipation of the increase in the value of the company resulting from the prospective takeover. This tactic makes the takeover unprofitable, since the premium accrues to the existing shareholders, rather than to the bidder. As a result, the potential bidder may withdraw the offer. Alternatively, the management may offer to buy back, at a premium, the shares already owned by the bidder. This practice is called "greenmail."

"Golden parachutes" (large severance payments offered to managers when their contracts are terminated) are sometimes mentioned on

---

63 U.S. courts have upheld the right of management to act in this fashion, on the grounds that it reflects "good business judgement." The business judgment rule excuses the officers or directors of a company from liability for any errors in judgment resulting in damages suffered by the firm, if the error was made in good faith and the decisions were based on sound business judgment of the officers or directors. For this defence to be accepted, it must be shown that the board of directors undertook a reasonable investigation and took appropriate action. Many of the scholars studying the application of the rule by U.S. courts concluded that the interests of shareholders have not been adequately safeguarded.

the list of takeover defences. However, as discussed in chapter 3, to the extent that they facilitate the replacement of incumbent managers, they should be viewed as a contribution to efficient allocation of resources. One complicating factor is that the cost of the golden parachutes may significantly contribute to the company debt. To guarantee their compatibility with shareholder interest, they should be approved by a majority vote.

The impact of the various anti-takeover defences is best seen in the context of our discussion of the economics of mergers and takeovers (chapter 3), the efficiency of the stock market (chapter 4), and its role in corporate governance (chapter 2). We have argued throughout that the benefits of the stock market for individual stockholders are maximized when stock markets are able to perform the full range of their functions.

In this section, we explained how anti-takeover defences limit shareholders in exercising their right of corporate ownership. Some of them aim at minimizing the influence of minority shareholders, but others are more general. They protect the interests of incumbent managers, and inhibit change in corporate control. Our objection to their use derives from the observation that they reduce the potential efficiency gains from mergers and takeovers. We argued that the interests of managers do not necessarily coincide with those of the shareholders. In such situations, anti-takeover defences effectively transfer wealth from shareholders to management and are objectionable on ethical grounds as well.

Insider trading

The term "insider trading" carries the connotation of unequal access to information and hence tends to generate an instinctive negative reaction. The economic consequences of insider trading are, however, somewhat subtle and deserve a brief elaboration. Insider trading is defined as the buying and selling of a company stock by its managers or by traders with access to information not accessible to those who would normally be able to obtain and use it.[64] In most jurisdictions, insider

---

64 The Ontario Securities Commission defines as "insiders" two categories of

trading is illegal. For example, Ontario law makes it illegal for anyone to enter into a security transaction if they have taken advantage of inside information about the corporation which is not available to other people. Any recipient of such information is also deemed to have committed an offence (Sharpe, Alexander and Fowler, 1993, p. 399).

The defenders of insider trading point out that it reveals valuable information, and prohibiting it would prevent the discovery of the true market price of the stock. They also claim that insider trading does not necessarily damage the non-participants; in fact non-participants (outsiders) may benefit, while the insiders bear the risk.

A typical scenario of the argument in favour of insider trading runs as follows: In the absence of insider trading the stock price fluctuates through time, without any obvious trend, until the management decides to make public valuable information. Consider first the release of positive information. The outsider shareholders may have an incentive to sell the stock before the information is released, i.e. before the stock reaches its equilibrium value. With insider trading, however, the stock price would gradually rise as those in possession of positive private information buy the stock. The outsiders will not sell until equilibrium value is reached. The same scenario holds in reverse when the information is negative (Martin and Peterson, 1991, pp. 57-58; Sen, 1993, pp. 222-225).

Insider trading thus speeds up the stock price change in either direction and facilitates the resulting wealth transfer. Neither the continuing holders of the stock, nor those who independently decide to sell while insiders are buying, are harmed by the actions of the insiders. Those outsiders who decide to keep the stocks benefit from their appreciation in value; those who sell before the equilibrium value is reached benefit at least partially. When insiders engage in selling, outsiders may

---

traders. One category are the officers and directors of a corporation whose securities are traded on an organized exchange in Ontario. Another category are shareholders who own 10% or more of the firm's shares (such shareholders are known as "beneficial owners"). Both types of insiders must report any transactions they have made in the firm's shares within 10 days after the end of the month in which the transaction(s) occurred (Sharpe, Alexander and Fowler, 1993, p. 399).

respond to this signal by bailing out of the depreciating stock earlier than would be the case if insider trading did not take place. Most of the risk of this process is borne by the insiders who do the trading, since they typically buy and sell large volumes of shares and are uncertain how the market will respond.

Given this argument, prohibiting insider trading may be viewed as misguided, since the prohibition makes it impossible for some owners of information to benefit from it. In addition, since managers are prohibited from trading their firm's securities at will, they have to be compensated by higher salaries, the cost of which is passed on to consumers in the form of higher prices.

Despite its possible benefits, both for insiders and for outsiders (non-participants), Werhane (1991) considers insider trading morally indefensible, because when managers buy and sell their company's stock, their interests may conflict with those of the rest of the shareholders. For example, instead of taking steps to correct the consequences of negligent performance of their responsibilities, managers may focus their effort on getting rid of the company stock before the potential negative impact of their mismanagement becomes known to the other shareholders.

In general, when insiders trade in the corporate stock, they are using shareholder property for their private gain. If the same information was available to other traders, it might affect their activity. In this sense, insider trading creates unfairness by "tilting the level playing field."

Insider trading also affects the process through which the final transaction price is established. This may reduce the efficiency of the stock market and thus impose costs on society (Sen, 1993, pp. 224-225). In the presence of insiders with superior information, outside traders tend to increase the "bid-ask spreads." As a result, fewer stocks are traded as the gap between the number of potential sellers and potential buyers grows larger. Since fewer stocks are traded, the potential economic benefits conferred by the stock market are reduced.

In order to enhance their chances, insiders may even manipulate the timing of crucial announcements made by the firm, possibly to the detriment of other stakeholders. An example is the alleged delaying of the announcement of assay results from mineral exploration programs by mining companies.

As is shown in chapter 4, insiders are able to make abnormal returns on their inside trades. Outsiders are also able to make abnormal returns by mimicking the trades of insiders, even with a lag. Insider trading is a high profile activity, since it is easily understood and has the appearance of unfairness. Many of the criticisms of the Vancouver Stock Exchange, for example, relate to insider trading activities. Similarly, the scandals on Wall Street in the 1980s prominently featured the insider trading violations of Dennis Levine, Ivan Boesky, and Foster Winans.

It has been argued that prohibitions on insider trading would weaken the pressure on managerial performance, since managers are not exposed to the risk of falling share prices. However, an efficient and well-functioning board of directors should devise a system of incentives ensuring that managers discharge their fiduciary responsibility to shareholders. Allowing managers to operate in a risk-free environment is as unethical and inefficient as insider trading (Werhane, 1991, p. 730). We discuss further the regulation of insider trading in chapter 7.

One approach to aligning the interests of management with the interests of outside shareholders is to encourage stock ownership by managers, for example, by introducing stock options as a component of managerial compensation. Typically, the option represents the right to buy the company stock at a stated price (usually the market price at the time when the option was granted). Alternatively, managers may be compensated in the form of "stock appreciation rights", i.e. based on the difference between the market price of the stock at the time of compensation and some previously stipulated benchmark price.

Ownership of shares and stock options by managers is effective in aligning their interests with those of the outside contributors of corporate capital only if there is some guarantee that the managers will retain the securities at least until such time as the relevant decisions are made (Barnea et al., 1985, pp. 97-99).

Conclusions

This chapter has examined some of the ethical issues related to the functioning of the stock market. We conclude that anti-takeover devices that prevent desirable mergers interfere with the ownership rights of shareholders and constitute an obstacle to efficient reallocation of resources.

The consequences of mergers and takeovers may include redistribution of income, closing of some plants and expansion of others, and elimination of specific managerial and other positions and creation of others. We argue that attempts to prevent the negative consequences by restricting takeovers are misguided and undermine the long-term growth of the economy. The same objection applies to attempts to restrict liquidating buyouts, since regulations constraining the actions of new owners might prevent them from remedying the shortcomings of the previous management.

Our review of the various anti-takeover defences concludes that they tend to favour the interests of managers over those of shareholders. In those cases where a company becomes a target of a liquidating takeover attempt because of a temporary excess of the breakup value of its assets over market value of its shares, anti-takeover defences may be ethically permissible. The justification for their use rests on the support of the majority of shareholders and on the demonstration that preservation of the integrity of the company is in the long-term interest of shareholders.

We have also dealt with the problem of informational asymmetry, which arises in situations where some agents (e.g. managers and other insiders) become knowledgeable about important corporate developments sooner than others (e.g. minority shareholders). Management buyouts and insider trading are among the most frequently discussed instances of informational asymmetry in the functioning of the stock market.

We conclude that the case for regulatory intervention is not overwhelming, since market participants without access to private information are capable of inferring its content from the actions of the insiders and the resulting changes in share prices. In our view, the current Canadian regulatory standards strike approximately the right balance between the interests of economic efficiency and ethical concerns for stakeholders with limited access to information. We address the regulatory issues more directly in the next chapter.

Chapter 7: Whither Regulation?

Introduction

THE OVERSEEING OF STOCK MARKETS in Canada is mostly a self-regulatory process. While in principle the activities of participants are regulated by provincial securities commissions, these bodies have typically delegated much of their authority to the exchanges and to the Investment Dealers Association. Bond dealers, broker-dealers (although to a limited extent, to be discussed later), and mutual funds dealers are also self-regulated. Regulation in general covers three sets of activities: prosecution of fraud, registration of market participants, and registration of traded securities (Hatch and Robinson, 1989).

Many stock market critics have called for stricter regulation and other forms of government intervention, citing a variety of shortcomings of the present system. An example of the prevailing hostile attitude to stock markets is contained in a recent report by the Economic Council of Canada

> At the same time, the dangers of unbridled competition must also be recognized. Safeguards must be put into place to support the continued solvency of our institutions, to strengthen the stability of markets, and to protect the consumers of financial

> services. Several recommendations [of the report] are aimed at achieving those goals.[65]

Much of this attitude results from not understanding the way that financial markets operate and the benefits they confer. We hope that this book will help educate interested parties in this regard. As well, many critics fail to realize that regulation has costs as well as supposed benefits.

If one attempts to distil the rhetoric of many of these critics, it becomes evident that there are two types of purported deficiencies in the present system: market failure and moral failure. Examples of supposed market failure include shareholder myopia (such as the alleged preference for short-term profits rather than investment in R&D, with the ensuing impairment of international competitiveness), market inefficiency (which erodes investor confidence and impairs economic growth), and the market's deficiencies in allocating capital for social as opposed to private profit-making objectives.[66] Examples of moral failure include the many instances of broker malfeasance that have unfortunately littered the history of stock markets, and which taint the ethical and legal activities of the majority of participants.

If valid, these criticisms would have serious implications for investor confidence (which in turn threatens the integrity of the capital formation process) and thus economic growth and global competitiveness. The remedies sometimes suggested for market failure include a stronger government role in capital allocation and in corporate gover-

---

65 "Globalization and Canada's Financial Markets," Economic Council of Canada, 1989, p. 120.

66 It is also often alleged that markets have become too volatile in recent years, largely as a result of trading in derivative securities. We show in chapter 1 that allegations of derivative-induced volatility have no empirical support. Kupiec (1991) shows further that there is no evidence of increasing sustained volatility in the major OECD equity markets over the past thirty years, with the short periods of abnormally high volatility that were experienced being quickly followed by a return to more "normal" levels. He also criticizes the remedies proposed to curtail the apparent problem, such as circuit breakers, transactions taxes, and margin requirements.

nance. Moral failure is said to require stricter regulation. This chapter reviews the evidence on these apparent failings and makes recommendations on the appropriate role of government in the control and functioning of stock markets.

Specifically, we show that the market is better suited to making capital investment decisions than is government, and that better enforcement rather than more regulation is needed for industry supervision. We will also examine a two-tier regulatory system that allows freer access to capital for more established firms while affording investor protection in the more speculative junior capital sector.

Market Failure

Market myopia and competitive disadvantage

Porter (1992) is one of the leading proponents of the myopic market theory (discussed in chapter 2). The argument is that investors with short holding periods pressure management to take short-term profit-maximizing actions, to the detriment of longer-term strategic investments, for example in research and development and in human capital. The lack of investor interest in strategic investments means that their cost of capital is too high and the competitiveness of firms subject to the pressures of myopic markets is undermined (see Pecaut, 1993, and figure 10 in chapter 4).

Among the remedies recommended by Pecaut and others (see chapter 4) are various types of government intervention. For example, Pecaut claims that governments can lengthen investor horizons through tax measures, such as selective capital gains relief, extended tax credits for research and development and for training costs, and other tax measures including incentives for venture capital companies. Alternatively, governments can support targeted stock savings plans offering tax relief to investors, implement changes in the regulation of banks to permit more keiretsu-style corporate organizations (the Japanese model, where banks and industrial corporations have much closer ties than in North America), or create a state-owned "Bank of Industrial Organization" to serve as a main bank for innovation-based businesses.

Pecaut recognizes the difficulties with many of these remedies, particularly with changes in the regulation of banks and the formation of an industrial bank. In the longer term, the onus is on the private sector to develop the institutional framework to solve these problems. Two areas with particular promise are the development of new financial institutions and the improvement of relations between providers and users of capital (discussed below). With respect to the tax-based remedies, the empirical evidence on their efficacy is mixed. Suret (1994) shows that the various activities of the Quebec government in intervening in the investment process have been wasteful, inefficient and unnecessary.

There is also evidence that the problem may be overstated or the blame misdirected. Johnson and Pazderka (1993) demonstrate that Canada is not disadvantaged relative to the United States as far as the myopic behaviour of the stock market is concerned. Jog and Srivastava (1993) show that the wedge between internal and external funding (which reduces the aggregate amount of corporate investment) is more a matter of corporate behaviour than evidence of market failure; that is, many corporate financiers have an aversion to raising new capital despite the small incremental cost.

The solution to market myopia (if indeed it is a problem) rests with the private sector. The financial reorganization recommended by both Pecaut and by Jog and Srivastava seems to be already evolving as the fallout from the financial market deregulation that began in the 1980s continues. As an illustration, the Canadian bank-owned brokerage houses are approaching the critical size necessary for global competitiveness. Meanwhile, the venture capital industry is increasingly meeting the needs of smaller, innovative companies, which traditionally have not had access to stock market financing.

There is scope for more private sector involvement in corporate finance and corporate governance if various financial regulations are relaxed. MacIntosh and Daniels (1990) discuss the impact of the "three 10% rules." The first of these is the regulation in the Income Tax Act that constrained (at that time) pension fund holdings of foreign assets to ten percent of the book value of the portfolio. Since domestic investment opportunities are limited, pension fund managers frequently cannot sell

Canadian stocks and are thus unable to voice disapproval of corporate management by "voting with their feet." That regulation has been relaxed somewhat, and pension funds may now hold up to 20 percent of their assets in foreign holdings. Ironically, this helps to make Canadian markets more effective since it gives the pension funds more choice and enhances their liquidity.

The second confining rule is the Bank Act constraint on ownership of Schedule A banks that restricts the maximum ownership of a bank by any one shareholder to ten percent. This results in less market discipline over bank management and the consequent reduced incentive for bank management to actively monitor their corporate clients.

The third confining regulation is the Bank Act prohibition on a bank's owning more than ten percent of a company. This limits both the incentive and the ability of bank managers to monitor their corporate investments. If they were allowed more concentrated ownership positions, they could exert more influence (and would have the incentive to do so).

There is evidence of a growing awareness of the implications of potential market myopia, as large institutional investors in both Canada and the U.S. are becoming increasingly interested in what has become known as "relationship investing." Institutional investors, such as Stephen Jarislowsky in Canada, and many of the larger American firms, are beginning to understand not only their power over corporate governance, but also their responsibility for more stable, partnership-like arrangements with the companies in which they invest. As noted in chapter 2, the Toronto Stock Exchange has recently established a Committee on Corporate Governance in Canada to study and make recommendations for improvement. Recent corporate restructuring and the turnover of senior officers at such companies as IBM, Sears, General Motors and Eastman Kodak can be attributed to institutional shareholder activism.

Market efficiency and investor confidence

Most of the deviations from market efficiency in Canada relate to insider trading (see chapter 4). Insider trading prevents the market from being efficient (in the sense of prices reflecting all information), since corporate insiders can make abnormal returns on their trades (Suret and Cormier, 1990). As well, it appears that opportunities for profits persist even after announcement of insider trades (Sharpe, Alexander, and Fowler, 1993), which implies that markets are slow to digest this particular form of information. This inertia tends to be clustered in industries which are not closely followed by professional analysts. Hence, there may be instances where a retail investor may be disadvantaged through lack of information (even though that information is available if anybody cared to look for it).

Does this evidence of information on insider trades not being reflected quickly in stock prices call for regulatory remedy? The natural response is the well-worn principle of *caveat emptor*: retail investors investing on their account (that is, not through a pooled fund such as a mutual fund) should either restrict their investments to more closely scrutinized companies, or should undertake to investigate and analyze the target companies by themselves. To the extent that retail investors may need additional protection, the two-tier market system discussed below in the section on moral failure should be adequate.

The social allocation of capital

It is sometimes stated that the invisible hand has no soul,[67] and as a consequence free markets will not undertake some socially desirable investments because private investors cannot capture enough of the benefits. Stock markets, according to this view, are therefore unable to assess such investments; that is, the capital formation process can fail for some socially desirable projects, and the government may be called upon to intervene for the good of society.[68] This form of intervention is not regulation per se (the subject of this chapter), but the issue naturally falls here under the broad discussion of alleged market failures.

---

67 This is of course an overstatement; examples of the market's "soul" include the so-called "green" investment funds.

68 This is not the same phenomenon as government direct investment in competitive enterprises (such as Petro Canada), for which there is usually some other political agenda.

What supporters of government investment do not realize is that there are costs other than the out-of-pocket expenses of administering such programs. These include "the opportunity cost of the restrictions imposed on the efficiency of financial markets, the opportunity cost of lessened economic growth which in turn results from directing savings toward projects on the basis of social return as opposed to economic return, and, in certain cases, the redistributional effects which work to the detriment of low-income families" (Van Horne, 1984, p. 273).

Van Horne concludes that government intervention in the capital allocation process often leads to lesser efficiency and lower economic growth, especially because of interference with the tradeoff between risk and return:

> The mechanism by which funds are channelled is the tradeoff between expected return and risk. When the government explicitly directs funds to certain investments which would either not be able to attract funds on their own or would attract them only at a higher rate of interest, it tampers with the workings of the marketplace. This tampering can lead to less efficient financial markets with the result that savings are allocated at higher costs and/or with greater inconvenience. This has adverse implications for us all. (Van Horne, p. 294)

This is not to say that capital markets are omnipotent or that there is no room for government involvement in socially desirable investments. However, the costs of such intervention must be carefully measured, and their broader implications for market efficiency and economic growth considered.

Moral Failure

The problem

Stock markets today are much more closely regulated than in their earlier history, especially prior to the crash of 1929, and most of the evils characterizing early markets no longer exist. Early in this century, pools of investors formed in the U.S. to manipulate prices through "wash sales" (non-arm's-length trades designed to give the impression of broader interest) and "corners" (a practice of purchasing a sufficient quantity of the float so that short sellers would be squeezed).[69] As a result, smaller investors were severely disadvantaged. At the same time, smaller investors were encouraged to over-invest in the stock market through virtually unlimited margin. This situation exacerbated the stock market crash of 1929, as investors had to dump their stock to meet margin calls.

The crash of 1929 led to the sweeping U.S. legislative reforms of the 1930s: the Securities Act of 1933, and the Securities Exchange Act of 1934. These laws established the Securities and Exchange Commission, provided for full public disclosure, banned manipulation, initiated registration of new securities issues, and established the concept of self-regulation by stock exchanges. The Bank Act of 1933 (better known as the Glass-Steagall Act) separated the banking and underwriting functions (Sloane, 1980, pp. 47-48).

Reform came to Canadian markets much later. Manipulation was still common in mining securities through the 1940s and 1950s, and "boiler rooms" (high pressure penny stock salespeople, the progenitors of today's broker-dealers) were active. There were no filing requirements for insider trading, and wash trades were common if not exactly legal. The Windfall Oils & Mines scandal of 1964, in which Viola MacMillan was accused of stock manipulation and wash sales, and convicted of the latter offence, led to the formation of a royal commission and a subsequent tightening of regulation of common stocks on the Toronto Stock Exchange in 1966 (Wells, 1991).

Many of the leading resource stock investors, led by Murray Pezim, then turned their attention to the Vancouver Stock Exchange. The book *The Pez* (Wells, 1991) provides detailed examples of the quasi-legal dealings of these speculators, such as manipulation, wash sales and

---

69 Short sellers sell shares of stock which they do not own (typically their broker lends the stock to them) in the hope that share prices will drop, at which time the short sellers would purchase the now cheaper stock and replace the borrowed stock. In a corner, there is little or no stock available for the short sellers to purchase, so they will pay any sum to cover their short position.

"backdooring" (advising clients to buy, while simultaneously selling on own account). The VSE has frequently been criticized by domestic commentators, notably by Diane Francis of the *Financial Post*; eventually, the international media began to spotlight some of these practices, and critical stories appeared in *Barron's* and *Forbes* (which labelled the VSE the "scam capital of the world"), and on U.S. television.

Recently, the British Columbia Securities Commission conducted a detailed review of the VSE's operations with a view to cleaning up its international image. The chairman of the commission, Douglas Hyndman, identified the major problems as: quality of listings; unsubstantiated ventures in fads; the conduct of directors, officers, and promoters; and the conduct of brokers.[70]

The interim report of the review revealed that most of the investors who were surveyed believe that the companies listed on the VSE are "products more of promotion than substance," that "the VSE operates for the benefit of its members rather than investors," and that "the only way to make money on the VSE is with insider information."[71] The areas for improvement suggested by investors include "more and clearer factual disclosure, non-voting public directors on company boards, a securities ombudsman, stricter penalties and enforcement, immediate insider reporting and declaration of all short positions, improved broker conduct and more effective and accessible civil remedies."[72]

The final report, issued by the chairman, James Matkin, in January 1994, recommended a sweeping overhaul of the "scandal-plagued" VSE, including a reduction in the power of the exchange and a reorganization of the B.C. Securities Commission. One of the focal points of the report was that "knowledge is power," and that the information the investors receive is flawed and not timely. Among the recommendations to redress this balance is the requirement that insider trades be published daily. The report concluded, however, that "the VSE is a

---

70 The *Globe and Mail*, July 14, 1993, p. B11.

71 The *Globe and Mail*, October 15, 1993, p. B3.

72 *Ibid.*

speculative market and responsible regulation should not and cannot protect the public from every misadventure . . . ; investors should always obey the injunction, 'caveat emptor.'"[73]

The VSE, not surprisingly, refutes many of these charges and asserts that they largely reflect past practice. VSE President Donald Hudson notes that "the exchange has sharply raised the standards of performance that it demands from brokers,"[74] and has instituted a record number of sanctions against member firms and employees for breaching securities regulations. In addition, new rules require sponsoring brokers to monitor new listings for one year, and to report any irregularities to the Exchange. The VSE was also the first North American exchange to computerize, and its computers are designed to detect any suspicious trading patterns (such as wash sales and backdooring). Hudson states that the true market test is the number of successful companies that have listed on the Exchange, of which there are numerous examples.

In Ontario, the topics currently on the regulatory reform agenda include a tighter definition of "frontrunning" (trading with the knowledge of an imminent trade likely to move the market—a form of insider trading) and renewed calls to limit the activities of broker-dealers. Broker-dealers deal in penny stocks, and their trades often represent the entire market. They do not belong to the Canadian Investor Protection Fund (which protects investors against a brokerage collapse), nor do they have strict self-regulatory discipline. The concern is that investors may not be able to differentiate between broker-dealers and regular stock brokers. The lack of clear distinction, according to the Investment Dealers Association, "ultimately harms the reputation of our capital markets."[75]

Other areas where investor protection has been called for are "churning" and insider trading. Churning is a practice where the broker

---

73 The *Globe and Mail*, January 26, 1994, p. B7.

74 *Maclean's* magazine, January 31, 1994, p. 34.

75 The *Financial Post*, November 13, 1992.

authorizes (in the case of discretionary accounts) or encourages an inordinate number of transactions in order to increase his or her commissions. Although illegal, prosecution for churning is slow and expensive, and the prospects for redress are limited. Many brokerage houses are moving away from transactions-based commissions to a system of flat, value-based fees, which should remove much of the incentive for churning. Insider trading remains a constant worry for regulators; U.S. regulators have recently enacted two new regulations to control the practice and to increase penalties (Gillis and Ciotti, 1992). Increased regulation in such areas as margin trading have also been called for (Singh and Talwar, 1987).

Some solutions

Whose interests are served by regulation? The principal players are investors, listed companies, brokers, and regulators, and it is instructive to consider their respective roles. There is an inherent tension between the need for investor protection and the need to "provide a supportive environment for business financing through accommodating primary markets anchored by an active secondary market" (Francis and Kirzner, 1988, p. 89). The capital formation process depends on investor confidence in the integrity of the system; its absence will lead to potential investors not investing, and economic growth suffering.

Standing between the investor and the company is the broker (see chapter 1 for a description of the broker's role in capital formation). Brokers are constrained by regulation, but at the same time they benefit from regulation in that (in most instances) it is impossible or at the least very difficult for investors to trade or for companies to raise new capital without using the services of brokers.

What about regulators? It could be argued that they are dispassionate agents of society who derive no inherent benefit from their role. However, like most public agencies, survival and growth are primary goals, and the maintenance and enhancement of the regulatory role tend to drive policy decisions. To a certain extent, regulators regulate because they like to regulate. Regulators also regulate because they have always done so: many regulations persist out of inertia and not from a continuing review of their ongoing usefulness. In the case of derivative securities, governments may have a concern that such securities remove control of cherished policy variables such as interest and exchange rates, since derivatives are created and traded largely outside the traditional system. As well, some governments are reacting to the supposed increase in the volatility of financial markets allegedly induced by derivatives, a phenomenon for which there is little empirical support (as we discussed in chapter 1).

Should stock markets be more tightly regulated? As Peter Drucker has been known to say, government should control the climate and not the weather. The previous section has shown that problems do exist, but many of them are a matter for better enforcement, not more regulation. Many critics have called for a centralization of securities regulation under federal jurisdiction in order to reduce duplication and to improve consistency; Daniels (1992) provides a critique of such recommendations and suggests that a modified provincial regulation system (described below) would be more effective.

There are instructive parallels between the regulation of stock markets and the regulation of public utilities. In both cases, protection of consumer interest is a paramount stated concern. In the case of public utilities, a regulatory revolution has taken place in the last decade as formerly regulated monopolistic lines of business (such as long distance telephone service) have been opened to competition, and the nature of regulation of the remaining regulated businesses (such as local exchange service) has been altered. U.S. and Canadian regulatory bodies (for example, the Federal Communications Commission and the Canadian Radio-Television and Telecommunications Commission, respectively) have recognized that regulation is not needed in the face of the force of competition, and that excess regulation can stifle innovation and productivity. The solution in the regulated utility industry has been a move toward incentive rate-of-return schemes (which reward efficient management) and away from strictly mechanistic cost-based regulation (which punishes efficient management).

The analogy in securities markets would be to have the degree of regulation dependent on the extent of "competition." In this context, competition is defined with respect to access to information, since, as discussed in chapter 4, information is the key to market efficiency. As in the case of evolving utility regulation, a residual level of investor protection is important to ensure confidence in the integrity of the system.

One interesting approach toward deregulation has been advocated by Daniels who envisions a two-tiered capital market (Daniels, 1992; MacIntosh and Daniels, 1990). The first tier would be populated by large, widely-followed companies whose securities are held by large, sophisticated institutional investors. The second tier would consist of smaller, more obscure companies and a larger number of less sophisticated retail investors. In the first tier, regulation is broadly unnecessary due to the sophistication of investors and the quantity of available information. In the second tier, a greater degree of regulation would be required.

In support of this model, MacIntosh and Daniels refer to the evidence on semi-strong form efficiency in Canada, where deviations from efficiency typically occur in those companies which are not widely followed by professional analysts. They also note that the lack of institutional investors in the second tier exposes retail investors to a higher risk of "predatory conduct" (actions taken by managers and inside shareholders to the detriment of outside shareholders).

The existence of a *de facto* two-tier market was recently acknowledged by the Toronto Stock Exchange (TSE), which began publicizing two new indexes: the TSE 100, comprising the largest 100 stocks on the TSE and designed to act as a benchmark for institutional investors; and the TSE 200, the smaller companies in the TSE 300, comprising more junior companies which typically lack the float or trading volume attractive to large institutional investors. In their news release of September 2, 1993, exchange officials touted the TSE 100 as providing "a more appropriate index for institutional performance since it contains an accurate list of the names of securities that large institutional investors can trade without size or liquidity limitations," while the TSE 200 was described as being "of use to equity fund managers interested in smaller-cap stocks." Haynes (1993) discusses the superiority of the TSE 100 over the TSE 35 and TSE 300 in the way it better reflects institutional activity.

There is already a degree of market segmentation in such activities as private placements, which are designed for larger investors and hence have less stringent disclosure requirements, and the use of prompt offering prospectuses (POPs). POPs were initiated in 1983 as a means of simplifying the disclosure requirements for new issuers of capital. Much of the information normally required by a prospectus can be pre-filed on an annual basis, and the company can then file simply the marginal information necessary at the time of a new share issuance. This considerably reduces the time to approve the issuance. This short form prospectus has been limited to larger companies with a history of reporting information.

The application of this model could take various forms. For example, the companies listed on a particular stock exchange could be separated by size and degree of information available, and regulated accordingly. This form of two-tier regulation has been proposed for the Canadian over-the-counter market, which comprises a mix of unlisted "blue chip" companies and unproven "penny stocks." "The top tier stocks would be those that meet tougher financial disclosure requirements, like minimum capital and net asset value numbers. The second tier would be the riskier stocks that don't."[76]

Alternatively, different exchanges could be regulated differentially, based on the same factors. In this latter model, the VSE, for example, would have more stringent reporting and disclosure requirements than would the TSE. A variant of this model was suggested anonymously to James Matkin during his review of the VSE: the suggestion was made that the province of British Columbia should set up "a competing exchange, one of clear and unquestionable integrity,"[77] which would fight it out with the existing VSE for business. One benefit of this approach would be to separate investors (who enter the market for long-term gain based on fundamental economic prospects) from gamblers (who have a short-term trading mentality).

---

76 The *Financial Times*, October 30, 1993, p. 13.

77 *Maclean's*, op. cit., p. 35.

The benefit of this two-tier system is that it allows larger companies more unfettered access to capital markets, while still providing access to capital by smaller, newer companies. On the investor side, the retail investor would be afforded protection where it is most likely to be efficacious, while the institutional investor would be better suited for self-protection.

Summary

This chapter has examined the alleged failures of the stock market and the appropriate level of regulatory response. With respect to the market failures, we conclude that the market is better suited than government to remedy any deficiencies in capital investment decisions. With respect to the moral failures, we conclude that better enforcement and not more regulation are needed; the two-tier market system we recommend would lead to less regulation for more established firms, and would focus investor protection where it is needed, in the more junior ventures.

Conclusions

WE CONCLUDE THAT STOCK MARKETS are an essential part of a market economy, and provide important "social benefits." The scope of our analysis has been far from exhaustive, yet we are confident that our assessment stands up to scrutiny. We have examined many of the principal activities of stock markets in some detail, and hopefully managed to debunk some myths and correct some popular misperceptions.

To set the scene, we first outlined the history and structure of stock markets, reviewed developments in new financial innovations, and discussed some of the pertinent current and evolving issues. We showed that stock markets perform a central role in the process of economic growth by bringing together groups of investors and matching them with companies needing capital in such a way that investors are able to satisfy their preferred mix of risk and reward while the best investment projects of competing companies are financed.

We then examined several aspects of the stock market's role in corporate governance as one of its social benefits. Ownership of a company's stock confers, in theory, control over the company's activities, thus providing a role for shareholders to exercise discipline over managerial self-interest.

Chapter 2 focused on the separation of ownership and control in shareholder-owned corporations and on differential voting shares. Both of these institutional features of corporate structure are frequently seen as weakening the ability of investors to fully exercise their ownership rights. In the parlance of economic theory, managers find it possible to engage in "non-value maximizing behaviour," i.e., pursue their own goals, sometimes to the detriment of shareholders. The various corrective mechanisms shareholders have at their disposal include takeover threats, discussed in chapter 3.

The other side of the coin is the danger that investors may be too impatient and put unreasonable pressure on managers to deliver high profits, quarter after quarter, possibly at the expense of the long-term prosperity of the corporation and the economy at large. The alleged myopia of institutional shareholders, in particular, has been widely suggested as a prime reason for the decline of North American industry.

We argued that the importance of this phenomenon may be overstated, and that at any rate, institutional shareholders have recently been moving toward a "relationship investing" role with corporate managers, in which they take a more active part in guiding and pressuring managers to take actions consistent with the needs of shareholders. We also presented evidence that the market recognizes that shares with more votes should have more value, so that the disadvantages of differential voting shares are offset by the market's setting of differential prices.

We then turned in chapter 3 to one of the most contentious aspects of the stock market's role in corporate governance—the market for corporate control. Much of the economic and finance literature views the stock market as a fundamental corrective mechanism ("a huge voting booth") through which owners assert their control over managers. Our discussion of mergers and takeovers confirms the validity of this characterization. Indeed, in our view, this function of stock markets, together with their prominence as a barometer of investor confidence, helps explain their pervasive influence over so many world economies. In most developed industrialized countries the share of stock markets in corporate financing is perhaps surprisingly low, as is evident from the statistics we presented in chapter 5. The influence wielded by stock price trends is much greater than the financing ratios would suggest—both for the management of a corporation whose share price takes a tumble, and for an economy whose leading stock market index changes direction.

The market for corporate control, and its chief instrument, the "hostile takeover," has evolved quite dramatically over the last two or three decades. The media, especially in the U.S., but also in Canada and elsewhere, have paid close attention to some of these developments. They raised the public awareness and profile of such financial innovations as "junk bonds," and of the tactics of "corporate raiders," their spectacular profits, and sometimes unethical or illegal practices. Unfortunately, the substantive economic impact of mergers and takeovers, and the social benefits accruing from the services of the stock market, have been much less well publicized and explained.

The point may have been lost that when deciding whether to make a bid, the acquiring managers presumably consider how they—and the merger—will add to the value of the target firm. Access to new markets or to capital, or improved position in the existing markets, technological synergy between the two firms, economies of scale and scope, possible tax advantages from combining a profit position of one firm with a loss position of the other, and, perhaps most importantly, replacement of a weak management team, are among the potential benefits for shareholders.

Managers of the bidding firms do, of course, pursue their own interests as well, and mergers and takeovers afford opportunities for promotion, control over larger staff, and increased managerial compensation, among others. The successful bidder often increases the corporate debt, reduces employment, and sells off parts of the target firm. In a hostile takeover, the bidder deals directly with shareholders of the target firm; their cooperation can only be assured by offering a premium (between 30 and 50 percent in recent experience) for their shares. Managers of the target firm are usually offered separation payments ("golden parachutes") to reduce their resistance to the takeover. The services of investment bankers, lawyers, and other experts assisting in the transaction are costly as well. On balance, however, takeovers do appear to add value to the economy.

Measurement of the efficiency gains resulting from takeovers is difficult, and an unknown portion of the benefits may be absorbed by the pursuit of managerial objectives and by the various types of transactions costs. An immense academic research effort has addressed the problem of identifying the sources and magnitude of benefits from mergers and takeovers, and their distribution among the various "stakeholders." While many of the findings are subject to debate, there are some reasonably robust conclusions based on U.S. and Canadian evidence: takeovers benefit the shareholders of the target companies; the gains to the shareholders of acquiring companies are much smaller, and from the 1980s on turned into losses; gains from economic efficiency resulting from takeovers (as distinct from tax savings, and other redistribution effects) increase the combined value of the acquired and acquiring companies; golden parachutes are not usually harmful to shareholders since they facilitate the transaction; and gains from takeovers do not generally result from increased monopoly power of the larger company resulting from the merger. As well, the fears that the threat of takeover encourages managers to focus attention on short-term financial results (behave myopically) to the detriment of R&D spending and other investments with longer payoff have not been substantiated by the evidence.

Careful academic analysis of leveraged buyouts, including those initiated by the incumbent management and financed by junk bonds, also yields a different picture than that painted by the mass media. When management owns a higher proportion of equity, the connection between ownership and control is restored. Managerial incentives are strengthened not only because of the ownership link, but also under pressure of the "discipline of debt," albeit in the form of junk bonds. Small companies sometimes issue junk bonds because they are cut off from bank financing, and the purchasers prefer the high-yielding bonds to equity claims in small and relatively unknown companies. Junk bonds thus satisfy needs of both lenders and borrowers which would otherwise be unsatisfied.

A direct measure of the stock market's social benefits is its ability to perform its "middleman" function. In chapter 4 we showed that the process of economic growth requires investor confidence, and that such confidence results from investor satisfaction with how well the market channels the investors' funds through to profitable investment opportunities. The market's performance in this respect is known as "efficiency."

Markets need to be efficient in both the external (prices reflect value) and the internal (they do so at low cost) sense. If the stock price does not represent the firm's value then investors are putting their money in the wrong place. If the cost of getting the stock price to reflect true value is too high, the economy suffers more mistaken investments. Canadian stock markets are global competitors and must be measured against global standards. In both senses, Canadian markets are similar to those of the U.S.: prices of common stocks are "fair" in most cases, and transaction costs are reasonable. Measured against Japan and Germany, Canada fares less well as the cost of capital in North America is typically higher than in those countries, which can impair global industrial competitiveness.

In applying an ethics perspective to stock market activities, we focused separately on two broad areas: mergers and takeovers, and cases of "moral failure" represented by malfeasance of traders.

We took the position that the overriding criterion of ethical behaviour in mergers, takeovers, and defences against hostile takeovers is the interest of shareholders, subject to the limits defined by the "loyal agent" concept. We examined, and found wanting, the objections against hostile buyouts based on their negative effects on some groups of stakeholders, the alleged resulting neglect of long-term investments, and the alleged disregard of moral duties associated with ownership.

The recent growth of stock markets in the developing and newly industrialized countries as well as in the former centrally-planned economies has far outstripped the trend in developed industrialized countries. This performance illustrates, once again, the unique advantages capital markets have over banks as a source of medium- and long-term risk financing in earlier stages of economic development and in periods of economic uncertainty—these advantages largely accruing from the spreading of risk among many shareholders as opposed to a bank assuming all risk. The disciplining function stock markets exert over management is of additional importance in these countries, where management talent even more scarce than in developed industrialized economies.

One of the themes frequently brought up throughout the book are the relative merits of the two main versions of shareholding. The first is characterized by the "Anglo-American" propensity of investors to treat share ownership as a means of gaining access to short-term returns.

They allow managers considerable autonomy, and quickly sell shares when there are signs that the firm is not doing well. A typical shareholder, even a big institution, typically holds only a small percentage of shares in any one company and trades them frequently. The exercise of shareholder control over management through shareholder vote and board of directors is weakened, and a remedial response has been the proliferation of takeovers and leveraged buyouts.

The second version of shareholding is sometimes described as "relationship investing," or as "Continental European-Japanese" corporate ownership. Here, investors take a long-term view and stay loyal to the firm, partly because several investors typically have a large stake. For example, many German firms have at least one shareholder—usually a bank, or a customer, or a supplier—with a stake exceeding 25 percent.[78] Not surprisingly, such shareholders take a much greater interest in corporate governance and are less likely to be accused of neglecting long-term investments in R&D, training of labour force and other "intangibles."

In several previous chapters we alluded to the controversy surrounding the connection between ownership structure and the comparative competitive performance of economies representing the two systems. Those who profess the superiority of "relationship investing" are tempted to recommend a fundamental redesign of the "Anglo-American" version of corporate ownership. A recent Canadian proposal, for example, speaks of "unleashing the latent power of the Canadian banking system," and encouraging the creation of a bank holding company with ability to engage in nonfinancial activities (Courchene, 1992).

The way in which such transformations are accomplished is of fundamental importance. Careful observers note that both of the major versions of corporate ownership are changing. Institutional investors in the "Anglo-American" system are less reluctant to take on larger stakes in a single firm, and a wide cross-section of investors have financed the growth of R&D-intensive firms in the drug industry, telecommunica-

---

78 "How to be a capitalist," *The Economist*, July 3, 1993, pp. 18-19.

tions, start-up software companies, etc. Changes are taking place in the other system as well. For example, German investors are increasingly questioning the close links between banks and industrial companies, there are growing pressures for enactment of a first German law banning insider trading, and shareholders are insisting on higher financial returns. In sum, "all dream of establishing in Germany the Anglo-Saxon equity culture in which shareholders rule."[79]

And whither regulation amidst all of this change? The most consistent critics of government interference remind us that regulators of capital markets tend to entrench the type of structure they are best familiar with. From this perspective, efforts to enact legislation against takeovers, or unnecessarily restrictive prohibitions on insider trading have the (intended or unintended) effect of protecting the incumbent management against shareholders. Restrictions on bank ownership in industrial enterprises fall into this category as well. The alternative is to allow the system to evolve, within limits, on the grounds that "capitalism has a knack of finding its own way."[80] We endorse this philosophical position. Our limits—given by the need to preserve investor confidence in the integrity of capital markets—are spelled out throughout the book.

---

79 "Learning to love equity," *The Economist*, July 3, 1993, p. 71.

80 "How to be a capitalist," *The Economist*, July 3, 1993, p. 19.

Glossary

Agency theory: a theory of corporate behaviour in which it is recognized that the manager, as agent, may have differing motives from the owner, as principal.

Arbitrage pricing theory (APT): an equilibrium model of stock returns in which returns are specified to be a linear function of possibly many factors, in contrast to the Capital Asset Pricing Model (CAPM), in which returns are specified to be a linear function of one factor, the systematic (non-diversifiable) risk.

Arbitrage traders: traders who seek price discrepancies for equivalent goods in different markets.

Blind pool: a type of investment fund initiated on the Alberta Stock Exchange in which the fund manager does not have to specify in detail the intended usage of the funds. Such funds were initially sold for five cents a share, hence the term "nickel shares."

Bought deal: a method of bringing corporate securities to the primary market in which the security dealer "buys" the entire issue and then resells it, in contrast to an "underwritten" deal in which the issue is largely committed for resale prior to its issuance.

Business Judgment Rule: in the absence of bad faith or some other corrupt motive, directors are normally not liable to the corporation for mistakes of judgment, whether those mistakes are classified as mistakes of fact or mistakes of law. The rule has functioned as a barrier to prevent courts from exercising regulatory powers over the activities of corporate managers.

Churning: excessive buying and selling of securities in a client's account so as to generate commissions.

Coat tail provision: a mechanism by which minority or lesser-voting shareholders are permitted to share in gains from a takeover. If an offer for some pre-specified amount (typically 50 percent) of the majority holding is made, the offer must be extended to the other shareholders (they ride the coat tails, as it were).

Common stock: a financial asset which represents an ownership claim on the issuing company. Stocks are traded either on stock exchanges or on electronic markets called over-the-counter markets.

Convertible bond: a bond that can be converted by the holder into some other asset, usually into common stock.

Derivative securities: financial assets whose value "derives" from the value of some underlying security or commodity. Examples include options and futures contracts.

Fiduciary constraint: a regulation that limits the investment options of institutions in a fiduciary (or trust) position with their clients. An example is the limitation on foreign assets which can be held in a pension plan.

Filter rules: a technical analysis strategy in which stocks are bought or sold after they have moved up or down by some predetermined amount (the filter).

Golden parachute: an attractive severance package for executives, especially those displaced by a takeover.

GPT ("going private transaction"): a transaction which transforms a publicly traded firm to a firm which is privately owned.

Greenmail: the act of acquiring a threatening equity position in a firm and then selling the equity to the existing owners at a premium.

Hedge: a strategy to offset investment risk. An example is the owner of a common stock who purchases a put option as insurance against a decline in the stock price.

Intermediation: the process of acting as a go-between. In financial markets, intermediation is between the suppliers and users of capital.

Junk bonds: original issue bonds rated as speculative grade.

LBO ("leveraged buyout"): a going private transaction in which the funds for the purchase are largely obtained through the issuance of debt, often "junk bonds." The purchasing group frequently includes incumbent managers.

LMBO ("leveraged management buyout"): a going private transaction financed by debt and led by corporate insiders.

MBO ("management buyout"): a going private transaction in which the buyers are dominated by corporate insiders.

Merger: a type of takeover where the bidder negotiates an agreement with management of the target firm on the terms of the offer for the target and then submits the proposed agreement to a vote of the shareholders.

Notional value: the face value of the underlying instruments on which derivatives are traded. For example, with a swap, the notional value would be the principal on the underlying loan.

Over-the-counter (OTC) markets: electronic trading systems for common stocks (in contrast to the physical stock exchanges). The Canadian Dealer Network is the major Canadian OTC market.

Preferred stock: a type of security which ranks between bonds and common stocks in priority of claims on the company.

Private placement: a type of primary security issue in which the securities are placed with a small number of large, "sophisticated," typically institutional, investors, thus bypassing the need for detailed prospectus disclosure.

Program trading: a kind of arbitrage between stock markets and stock index futures or options markets. A computer is programmed to detect price discrepancies between two markets and to initiate trades when discrepancies are found.

Proxy contest: a type of takeover where a dissident group attempts through a vote of shareholders to obtain control of the board of directors.

Relationship investing: the close governance of corporations exercised by large institutional shareholders.

Rights and warrants: financial assets which provide their holders with the option to purchase a specified number of shares at a specified price within a specified time period. Note the similarity with call options. Rights (preemptive rights) are initially issued to current owners of the underlying common stock. Warrants are usually issued as a sweetener for a bond or preferred share issue. When warrants are issued with new common stock, the package is called a unit.

Soft dollar services: non-transaction services offered by stock brokers. Examples include investment advice, economic forecasts, and research reports.

Stock exchange: a physical central market for the issuance and trading of common stocks, in contrast to the over-the-counter market, which is an electronic marketplace.

Swap: a type of derivative security wherein two or more parties contract to swap payments on each other's obligations. Examples include interest rate swaps, where fixed interest rates are swapped for floating interest rates, and currency swaps, where one currency is swapped for another.

Technical analysis: a type of equity investing in which stock price movements are predicted from charts or patterns of past price movements.

Tender offer: a type of takeover where the bidder makes an offer directly to shareholders to buy some or all of the stock of the target firm.

The tender offer is described as "friendly" if it is supported by target management and "hostile" if it is opposed by target management.

Tender offer premium: the amount by which a tender offer exceeds the pre-bid market price of the stock.

Toronto Index Participation Units (TIPs): artificial securities whose value depends on the price movements of the stocks comprising the TSE 35 Index.

Two-tier offer: a type of takeover where the bidder first makes an offer for control of the firm and then makes a "clean-up" offer for the remaining shares at lower price.

Underwriting: the process of bringing a new issue of securities to the market. In a traditional underwriting, the underwriter would form a syndicate of dealers who would pre-sell much of the issue prior to issuance. In a bought deal, the dealer buys the issue from the issuing company and then arranges buyers.

Venture capital: pools of investment money which typically are placed in the form of equity in start-up (usually risky) companies.

Bibliography

Abeysekera, Sarath and Arvind Mahajan. 1987. "A Test of the APT in Pricing Canadian Stocks." *Canadian Journal of Administrative Sciences* 4:186-198.

Allen, Franklin. 1993. "Stock Markets and Resource Allocation." In Collin Mayer and Xavier Vives, eds. *Capital Markets and Financial Intermediation.* Cambridge: Cambridge University Press, pp. 81-116.

Almeder, Robert and David Carey. 1991. "In defense of sharks. Moral issues in hostile liquidating takeovers." *Journal of Business Ethics* 10:471-484.

Amoako-Adu, Ben and Brian Smith. 1991. "How Do Shareholders Fare in Minority Buyouts?" *Canadian Investment Review* 4:79-86.

Andrews, A. Michael. 1991. *The Canadian Securities Industry: A Decade of Transition.* Conference Board of Canada Report, pp. 68-91.

_____. 1993. "Why Antiquated Backrooms Threaten the Existence of Canada's Capital Markets." *Canadian Investment Review* 6:13-17.

Baesel, Jerome and Garry Stein. 1979. "The Value of Information: Inferences from the Profitability of Insider Trading." *Journal of Financial and Quantitative Analysis* 14:553-569.

Barnea, Amir, Robert A. Haugen and Lemma W. Senbet. 1985. *Agency Problems and Financial Contracting*. Englewood Cliffs, N.J.: Prentice-Hall.

Baruch, Hurd. 1971. *Wall Street: Security Risk.* Baltimore: Penguin Books.

Baumol, William. 1965. *The Stock Market and Economic Efficiency*. New York: Fordham University Press.

Beck, Nuala. 1992. *Shifting Gears: Thriving in the New Economy*. Toronto: Harper Collins Publishers.

Ben-Zion, Uri. 1984. "The R&D and investment decision and its relationship to the firm's market value: Some preliminary results." In *R&D, Patents, and Productivity*. Zvi Griliches, ed. Chicago: University of Chicago Press.

Bernstein, Peter. 1992a. "Are Financial Markets the Problem or the Solution? A Reply to Michael Porter." *Journal of Applied Corporate Finance* 5:17-22.

_____. 1992b. *Capital Ideas: The Improbable Origins of Modern Wall Street*. New York: Macmillan.

Blundell-Wignall, Adrian, Frank Bowne, and Paolo Manasse, "Monetary Policy in Liberalised Financial Markets," *OECD Economic Studies*, No. 15, Autumn 1990, pp. 146-178.

Briloff, Abraham. 1988. "Cannibalizing the Transcendent Margin: Reflections on Conglomeration, LBOs, Recapitalizations and Other Manifestations of Corporate Mania." *Financial Analysts Journal* 44:74-80.

Brown, Ian. 1989. *Freewheeling*. Toronto: Harper Collins.

Calvet, A. Luis and Jean Lefoll. 1980. "The CAPM Under Inflation and the Performance of Canadian Mutual Funds." *Journal of Business Administration* 12:107-117.

_____. 1985. "The Market for Corporate Acquisitions in Canada." In William Rentz, ed., *Proceedings of the 1985 Administrative Sciences Association of Canada Conference*, pp. 192-205.

Calvo, Guillermo A. and Manmohan S. Kumar. 1993. "Financial Sector Reforms and Exchange Arrangements in Eastern Europe." *Occasional Paper 102*. Washington, D.C.: International Monetary Fund.

Canada. Statistics Canada. Annual. *Industrial Research and Development*. Cat. 88-202. Ottawa: Statistics Canada.

Canada. Consumer and Corporate Affairs Canada. Annual. *Report of the Director of Investigation and Research*. Ottawa: Supply and Services Canada.

Canadian Institute of Actuaries. Annual. *Report on Canadian Economic Statistics*. Ottawa: Canadian Institute of Actuaries.

Catte, Pietro and Cristina Mastopasqua. 1993. "Financial Structure and Reforms in Central and Eastern Europe in the 1980s." *Journal of Banking and Finance* 17: 785-817.

Chamberlain, Trevor, Sherman Cheung and Clarence Kwan. 1988. "Day of the Week Patterns in Stock Returns: The Canadian Evidence." *Canadian Journal of Administrative Sciences* 5:51-55.

_____. 1993. "Options Listing, Market Liquidity and Stock Behaviour: Some Canadian Evidence." *Journal of Business Finance and Accounting* 20: 687-698.

Charest, Guy. 1980. "Returns to Dividend Changing Stocks on the Toronto Stock Exchange." *Journal of Business Administration* 12:1-18.

Cooke, Gilbert W. 1969. *The Stock Markets*. Cambridge, Mass.: Schenkman Publishing.

Courchene, Thomas J. 1992. "Presidential Address: Mon pays, c'est l'hiver: Reflections of a Market Populist." *Canadian Journal of Economics* 25:759-791.

Cox, John and Mark Rubinstein. 1985. *Options Markets*. Englewood Cliffs, N.J.: Prentice-Hall.

Daniels, Ronald. 1992. "How 'Broke' is the System of Provincial Securities Regulation?" *Canadian Investment Review* 5:89-98.

DeAngelo, Harry and Linda DeAngelo. 1987. "Management Buyouts of Publicly Traded Corporations." *Financial Analysts Journal* 43:38-49.

Dice, Charles Amos. 1926. *The Stock Market*. New York: McGraw Hill.

EcoDiagnostic. 1993. "Financial Markets: Mission Impossible?" *Report No. 3*. Geneva: Fondation pour le Progrès de l'Homme.

Elias, Christopher. 1971. *Fleecing the Lambs*. Greenwich, Conn.: Fawcett Publications.

Ewin, Robert E. 1991. "The moral status of the corporation." *Journal of Business Ethics* 10:749-756.

Fama, Eugene. 1970. "Efficient Capital Markets: A Review of Theory and Empirical Work." *Journal of Finance* 25:383-417.

_____. 1991. "Efficient Capital Markets: II." *Journal of Finance* 46:1575-1617.

Fletcher, James. 1992. "Venture Capital in Canada: Redesigning the Pipeline." *Canadian Investment Review* 5:99-103.

Foerster, Stephen and David Porter. 1993. "Calendar and Size-Based Anomalies in Canadian Stock Returns." In Michael Robinson and Brian Smith, eds. *Canadian Capital Markets*, London: Western Business School, pp. 133-140.

Fowler, David, Harvey Rorke and Vijay Jog. 1980. "Thin Trading and Beta Estimation Problems on the Toronto Stock Exchange." *Journal of Business Administration* 12:77-90.

Francis, Jack and Eric Kirzner. 1988. *Investments Analysis and Management: First Canadian Edition*. Toronto: McGraw-Hill Ryerson.

Friedman, Milton. 1962. *Capitalism and Freedom*. Chicago: University of Chicago Press.

Gillis, John and Glenn Ciotti. 1992. "Insider Trading Update." *Financial Analysts Journal* 48:46-51.

Greenwald, John, "The Devil's in the Derivatives," *Time Magazine*, October 10, 1994, pp. 48-50.

Griffiths, Mark. 1993. "A Study of Systematic Changes in the Level of Investor Trading." In Michael Robinson and Brian Smith, eds., *Canadian Capital Markets*, London: Western Business School, pp. 29-43.

Grundfest, Joseph. 1993. "Zen and the Art of Securities Regulation." *Journal of Applied Corporate Finance* 5:4-8.

Hall, Bronwyn. 1990. "The Impact of Corporate Restructuring on Industrial Research and Development." *Brookings Papers on Economic Activity—Microeconomics* pp. 85-124.

Hatch, James and Michael Robinson. 1989. *Investment Management in Canada*. 2nd ed. Scarborough: Prentice-Hall Canada.

Hatch, James and Robert White. 1988. *Canadian Stocks, Bonds, Bills and Inflation: 1950-1987*. Charlottesville, Va.: Financial Analysts Research Foundation.

Hatch, James and Robert White. 1989. "Anatomy of a Stock Market Crash: The Case of October 1987." *Canadian Investment Review* 2:17-22.

Hayek, Friedrich H. 1945. "The Use of Knowledge in Society." *American Economic Review* 35:519-530.

Haynes, Peter. 1993. "100 Reasons for a New TSE Index." *Canadian Investment Review* 6:18-22.

Hennessey, Sean. 1993. "Can Active Managers Profit from Earnings Forecasts Revisions?" *Canadian Investment Review* 6:39-45.

Hughes, Patricia. 1984. "A Test of the Arbitrage Pricing Theory Using Canadian Security Returns." *Canadian Journal of Administrative Sciences* 1:195-214.

Hunter, William. 1986. *Canadian Financial Markets*. Peterborough: Broadview Press.

Jaffe, Jefferey and Randolph Westerfield. 1985. "The Weekend Effect in Common Stock Returns: The International Evidence." *Journal of Finance* 40:433-454.

Jarislowsky, Stephen, Jean-Claude Delorme, James Maunder, Ned Goodman, and Tullio Cedraschi. 1991. "Corporations and Institutional Investors: Five Key Players Look Ahead." *Canadian Investment Review* 4:17-24.

Jarrell, Gregg A., James A. Brickley and Jeffry M. Netter. 1988. "The Market for Corporate Control: The Empirical Evidence since 1980." *Journal of Economic Perspectives* 2:49-68.

Jensen, Michael. 1988. "Takeovers: Their Causes and Consequences." *Journal of Economic Perspectives* 2:21-48.

Jensen, Michael and William Meckling. 1976. "Theory of the Firm: Managerial Behavior, Agency Costs and Ownership Structure." *Journal of Financial Economics* 3:305-360.

Jog, Vijay. 1986. "Investment Performance of Pension Funds: A Canadian Study." *Canadian Journal of Administrative Sciences* 3:146-163.

_____. 1988. "Stock Pricing Anomalies: Canadian Experience." *Canadian Investment Review* 1:55-62.

Jog, Vijay and Allan Riding. 1986. "Price Effects of Dual-Class Shares." *Financial Analysts Journal* 42:58-67.

_____. 1987. "Underpricing in Canadian IPOs." *Financial Analysts Journal* 43:48-55.

Jog, Vijay, Alan Riding and Paul Seguin. 1985. "Shareholders' Reactions to Issuances of Restricted Voting Common Stock." In William Rentz (ed.), *Proceedings of the 1985 Administrative Sciences Association of Canada Conference* (Finance Division), pp. 10-18.

Jog, Vijay and Ashwani Srivastava. 1993. "How Capital Formation Hinders Canada's Competitiveness Against Foreign Firms." *Canadian Investment Review* 6:21-26.

Johnson, Lewis D. and Edwin H. Neave. 1994. "Governance and Competitive Advantage." *Managerial Finance* (forthcoming).

Johnson, Lewis D. and Bohumir Pazderka. 1993. "Firm Value and Investment in R&D." *Managerial and Decision Economics* 14:15-24.

Joint Securities Industry Committee. 1984. *Regulation and Ownership of Market Intermediaries in Canada.* Report of the Joint Securities Industry Committee on behalf of the Alberta, Montreal, Toronto, and Vancouver Stock Exchanges and the Investment Dealers Association of Canada.

Jones, Thomas M. and Reed O. Hunt. 1991. "The ethics of leveraged management buyouts revisited." *Journal of Business Ethics* 10:833-840.

Kelley, David and Jeff Scott. 1993. "Gekko Echo." *Reason* 24:30-37.

Kirzner, Eric. 1990. "Stock Markets at the Crossroads: Where to from Here?" *Canadian Investment Review* 3:41-46.

_____. 1992. "The Toronto Stock Exchange's New Electronic World." *Canadian Investment Review* 5:83-88.

Krinsky, I. and Wendy Rotenberg. 1989. "The Valuation of Initial Public Offerings." *Contemporary Accounting Research* 5:501-515.

Kryzanowski, Lawrence. 1979. "The Efficacy of Trading Suspensions: A Regulatory Action Designed to Prevent the Exploitation of Monopoly Information." *Journal of Finance* 34:1187-1200.

Kryzanowski, Lawrence and Hao Zhang. 1993. "Market behaviour around Canadian stock-split ex-dates." *Journal of Empirical Finance* 1:57-81.

Kupiec, Paul, "Stock Market Volatility in OECD Countries: Recent Trends, Consequences for the Real Economy, and Proposals for Reform," *OECD Economic Studies*, No. 17, Autumn 1991, pp. 31-62.

Lawson, William. 1980. "Market Efficiency: The Trading of Professionals on the Toronto Stock Exchange." *Journal of Business Administration* 12:41-55.

Lewis, Michael. 1989. *Liar's Poker*. New York: Norton & Company.

Loomis, Carol J., "The Risk that Won't Go Away," *Fortune*, March 7, 1994.

MacIntosh, Jeffrey and Ronald Daniels. 1990. "Capital Markets and the Law: The Peculiar Case of Canada." *Canadian Investor Review* 3:77-84.

Markowitz, Harry. 1992. "Markets and morality." *Journal of Portfolio Management* 18:84-93.

Martin, Deryl W. and Jeffrey H. Peterson. 1991. "Insider trading revisited." *Journal of Business Ethics* 10:57-61.

Maynes, Elizabeth. 1991. "Evidence on the Value of a Stock Exchange Listing." *Canadian Journal of Administrative Sciences* 8:179-191.

Maynes, Elizabeth, Chris Robinson and Alan White. 1990. "How Much is a Share Vote Worth?" *Canadian Investment Review* 3:49-55.

McCauley, Robert and Steven Zimmer. 1989. "Explaining International Differences in the Cost of Capital." *Federal Reserve Bank of New York Quarterly Review*, pp. 7-28.

Meade, Nancy L. and Dan Davidson. 1993. "The use of 'shark repellents' to prevent corporate takeovers: An ethical perspective." *Journal of Business Ethics* 12:83-92.

Mitchell, Mark. 1991. "The Value of Corporate Takeovers." *Financial Analysts Journal* 47:21-31.

Mittoo, Usha. 1991. "Do Financial Markets Learn From Academic Research?" *Canadian Investment Review* 4:83-86.

Miurin, Paolo and Andrea Sommariva. 1993. "The Financial Reforms in Central and Eastern European Countries and in China." *Journal of Banking and Finance* 17: 883-911.

Morin, Roger. 1980. "Market Line Theory and the Canadian Equity Market." *Journal of Business Administration* 12:57-76.

Ney, Richard. 1970. *The Wall Street Jungle.* New York: Grove Press.

Otuteye, Eben. 1991. "How Economic Forces Explain Canadian Stock Returns." *Canadian Investment Review* 4:93-99.

Parker, David. 1993. "Unravelling the Planned Economy: Privatisation in Czecho-Slovakia." *Communist Economies & Economic Transformation* 5:391-404.

Pecaut, David. 1993. "Canada's High Cost of Capital: A Barrier to Investing for the Future." *Canadian Investment Review* 6:9-16.

PlanEcon. 1993. "East European Stock Market Report: Polish, Hungarian, and Czech Stock Markets Outperform Most Other Emerging Markets by a Wide Margin." *PlanEcon Report,* Vol. IX, Nos. 40-41, November 19, 1993. Washington, D.C.: PlanEcon, Inc.

Por, John. 1993. "A New Approach to Corporate Governance." *Canadian Investment Review* 6:33-38.

Porter, David. 1993. "Stock Splits and Changing Betas." In Michael Robinson and Brian Smith, eds., *Canadian Capital Markets,* London: Western Business School, pp. 141-152.

Porter, Michael. 1992. "Capital Choices: Changing the Way America Invests in Industry." *Journal of Applied Corporate Finance* 5:4-16.

Reilly, Frank. 1989. *Investment Analysis and Portfolio Management.* Chicago: Dryden Press.

Robinson, Chris and Walter Block. 1991. "Are Corporate Takeovers Good or Bad? A Debate." *Canadian Investment Review* 4:53-58.

Robinson, Chris and Alan White. 1991. "The Effect of a Change in Takeover Protection on Dual Class Equity." In Gordon Sick (ed.), *Proceedings of the 1991 Adninistrative Sciences Association of Canada Conference* (Finance Division), pp. 101-110.

Robinson, Michael. 1993a. "Raising High-Risk Equity Capital: Alberta's JCP Program." In Alex Faseruk, ed., *Proceedings of the Administrative Sciences Association of Canada Conference.*

_____. 1993b. "Univariate Canadian CAPM Tests." In Michael Robinson and Brian Smith, eds., *Canadian Capital Markets*, London: Western Business School, pp. 101-119.

Robinson, Michael and Robert White. 1991. "An Examination of the Canadian Block Trading Market." In Gordon Sick, ed., *Proceedings of the 1991 Administrative Sciences Association of Canada Conference*, pp. 151-160.

Ross, Alexander. 1984. *The Traders*. Don Mills: Collins Publishers.

Rotenberg, Wendy. 1990. "Pricing Initial Public Equity Offerings: Who Wins, Who Loses and Why?" *Canadian Investment Review* 3:17-23.

Scherer, Frederick M. 1988. "Corporate Takeovers: The Efficiency Arguments." *Journal of Economic Perspectives* 2:69-82.

Schulman, Evan. 1989. "The 'Global Village' Securities Market: Will Canada be a Participant . . . Or a Bystander?" *Canadian Investment Review* 2:61-66.

Shleifer, Andrei and Robert W. Vishny. 1988. "Value Maximization and the Acquisition Process." *Journal of Economic Perspectives* 2:7-20.

Sen, Amartya. 1993. "Money and Value—On the Ethics and Economics of Finance." *Economics and Philosophy* 9:202-227.

Sharpe, William, Gordon Alexander and David Fowler. 1993. I*nvestments: First Canadian Edition.* Scarborough: Prentice-Hall.

Singh, Saraswati and Prem Talwar. 1987. "Margin Requirements in the Security Market and Public Policy." *Canadian Journal of Administrative Sciences* 4:52-65.

Sloane, Leonard. 1980. *The Anatomy of the Floor*. New York: Doubleday and Company.

Smith, Brian. 1993. "A Study of the Arbitrage Pricing Theory Using Daily Returns of Canadian Stocks." In Michael Robinson and Brian Smith, eds., *Canadian Capital Markets*, London: Western Business School, pp. 121-131.

Srivastava, Ashwani. 1990. "An Evaluation of Flotation Costs of a Private Equity Placement." In Trevor Chamberlain, ed., *Proceedings of the 1990 Administrative Sciences Association of Canada Conference*, pp. 200-210.

Stewart, Walter. 1992. *The Golden Fleece*. Toronto: McClelland & Stewart.

Stoll, Hans. 1993. "Organization of the Stock Market: Competition or Fragmentation?" *Journal of Applied Corporate Finance* 5:89-93.

Suret, Jean Marc, "Le gouvernement du Québec et le financement des entreprises: les mauvais réponses à un faux problème," *L'état Interventionniste*, ed. Filip Palda (The Fraser Institute, 1994), pp. 113-168.

Suret, Jean-Marc and Elise Cormier. 1990. "Insiders and the Stock Market." *Canadian Investment Review* 3:87-90.

Tarasofsky, Abraham and Ronald Corvari. 1991. *Corporate Mergers and Acquisitions: Evidence on Profitability. A Study Prepared for the Economic Council of Canada*. Ottawa: Supply and Services Canada.

Tease, Warren, "The Stock Market and Investment," *OECD Economic Studies*, No. 20, Spring 1993, pp. 41-63.

Thain, Donald and David Leighton. 1991. "Ownership Structure and the Board." *Canadian Investment Review* 4:61-65.

Thorne, Alfredo. 1993. "Eastern Europe's Experience with Banking Reform: Is There a Role for Banks in the Transition?" *Journal of Banking and Finance* 17: 959-1000.

Van Horne, James. 1984. *Financial Market Rates and Flows*. Englewood Cliffs, N.J.: Prentice-Hall.

Walkling, Ralph and Robert Edmister. 1985. "Determinants of Tender Offer Premiums." *Financial Analysts Journal* 41:27-37.

Waitzer, Edward. 1991. "Are Institutional Investors Really Impacting Corporate Governance?" *Canadian Investment Review* 4:9-14.

Wells, Jennifer. 1991. *The Pez*. Toronto: Macfarlane Walter & Ross.

Werhane, Patricia H. 1991. "The indefensibility of insider trading." *Journal of Business Ethics* 10:729-731.

West, Richard. 1975. "On the Difference Between Internal and External Market Efficiency." *Financial Analysts Journal* 31:30-34.

White, Alan, Chris Robinson, and Gyan Chandra. 1985. "The Value of Voting Rights and Restricted-Voting Shares." In William Rentz, ed., *Proceedings of the 1985 Administrative Sciences Association of Canada Conference*, pp. 1-9.

Wolfe, Tom. 1987. *The Bonfire of the Vanities.* New York: Farrar, Straus, Giroux.

Woolridge, J. Randall. 1988. "Competitive Decline: Is a Myopic Stock Market to Blame?" *Journal of Applied Corporate Finance* 1:26-36.